Self-Analysis

K A R E N   H O R N E Y,   M. D.

The Norton Library NEW YORK
W · W · NORTON & COMPANY · INC ·

W. W. Norton & Company, Inc. is also the publisher of
the works of Erik H. Erikson, Otto Fenichel, Karen Horney and
Harry Stack Sullivan, and the principal works of Sigmund Freud.

PRINTED IN THE UNITED STATES OF AMERICA

2 3 4 5 6 7 8 9 0

CONTENTS

Psychoanalysis first developed as a method of therapy in the strict medical sense. Freud had discovered that certain circumscribed disorders that have no discernible organic basis—such as hysterical convulsions, phobias, depressions, drug addictions, functional stomach upsets —can be cured by uncovering the unconscious factors that underlie them. In the course of time disturbances of this kind were summarily called neurotic.

After a while—within the last thirty years—psychiatrists realized that neurotic people not only suffer from these manifest symptoms but also are considerably disturbed in all their dealings with life. And they also recognized the fact that many people have personality disorders without showing any of the definite symptoms that had previously been regarded as characteristic of neuroses. In other words, it gradually became more apparent that in neuroses symptoms may or may not be present but personality difficulties are never lacking. The conclusion was thus inevitable that these less specific difficulties constitute the essential core of neuroses.

The recognition of this fact was exceedingly constructive in the development of psychoanalytical science, not only increasing its efficacy but also enlarging its scope.

Manifest character disorders, such as a compulsive indecision, a repeated wrong choice of friends or lovers, gross inhibitions toward work, became as much an object of analysis as the gross clinical symptoms. Nevertheless the focus of interest was not the personality and its best possible development; the ultimate purpose was the understanding and eventual removal of the obvious disorders, and analysis of the character was only a means toward this end. It was almost an accidental by-product if in consequence of such work a person's whole development took a better course.

Psychoanalysis is still and will remain a method of therapy for specific neurotic disorders. But the fact that it can be an aid to general character development has come to assume a weight of its own. To an increasing degree people turn to analysis not because they suffer from depressions, phobias, or comparable disorders but because they feel they cannot cope with life or feel that factors within themselves are holding them back or injuring their relationships with others.

As will happen when any new vista is opened up, the significance of this new orientation was at first overrated. It was frequently declared, and the opinion is still widespread, that analysis is the only means of furthering personality growth. Needless to say, that is not true. Life itself is the most effective help for our development. The hardships that life forces upon us—a necessity to leave one's country, organic illness, periods of solitude—and also its gifts—a good friendship, even a mere contact with a truly good and valuable human being, co-operative

8

work in groups—all such factors can help us reach our full potential. Unfortunately, the assistance thus offered has certain disadvantages: the beneficent factors do not always come at the time we need them; the hardships may not only be a challenge to our activity and courage but surpass our available strength and merely crush us; finally, we may be too entangled in psychic difficulties to be able to utilize the help offered by life. Since psychoanalysis has not these disadvantages—though it has others —it can legitimately take its place as one specific means in the service of personal development.

Any help of this kind is made doubly necessary by the intricate and difficult conditions that we all live under in our civilization. But professional analytical help, even if it could be made available to more people, can scarcely reach everyone whom it is capable of benefiting. It is for this reason that the question of self-analysis has importance. It has always been regarded as not only valuable but also feasible to "know oneself," but it is possible that the endeavor can be greatly assisted by the discoveries of psychoanalysis. On the other hand, these very discoveries have revealed more than was ever known before about the intrinsic difficulties involved in such an undertaking. Therefore humility as well as hope is required in any discussion of the possibility of psychoanalytic self-examination.

It is the object of this book to raise this question seriously, with all due consideration for the difficulties involved. I have attempted also to present certain basic considerations regarding procedure, but since in this

‚field there is little actual experience to serve as guide my purpose has been primarily to raise the issue and to encourage endeavors toward a constructive self-examination rather than to offer any clear-cut answers.

Attempts at constructive self-analysis can be important, in the first place, for the individual himself. Such an endeavor gives him a chance for self-realization, and by this I mean not only the development of special gifts that he may have been inhibited from utilizing but also, even more important, the development of his potentialities as a strong and integrated human being, free from crippling compulsions. But there is also a broader issue involved. An integral part of the democratic ideals for which we are fighting today is the belief that the individual—and as many individuals as possible—should develop to the full of his potentialities. By helping him to do this psychoanalysis cannot solve the ills of the world, but it can at least clarify some of the frictions and misunderstandings, the hates, fears, hurts, and vulnerabilities, of which those ills are at once cause and effect.

In two earlier books I presented the framework of a theory of neuroses which I have elaborated in the present volume. I would gladly have avoided presenting these new viewpoints and formulations in this book, but it did not appear sensible to withhold anything that might be useful for self-examination. I have tried, however, to present matters as simply as possible without distorting the subject matter. The highly intricate nature of psychological problems is a fact that cannot and must not be disguised, but with full mindfulness of that intricacy I have tried not to increase it by a lumbering terminology.

I take this opportunity to express my thanks to Miss Elizabeth Todd for the astute understanding with which she has helped to organize the material. And I should like to thank my secretary, Mrs. Marie Levy, for her untiring efforts. I wish, too, to express my gratitude to the patients who have allowed me to publish their experiences in self-analysis.

CHAPTER ONE

Feasibility

and Desirability of Self-Analysis

Every analyst knows that an analysis proceeds the more quickly and efficiently the more the patient "co-operates." When speaking of co-operation I have not in mind the patient's polite and obliging acceptance of whatever the analyst suggests. Nor am I referring primarily to the patient's conscious willingness to give information about himself; most patients who come to analysis of their own accord sooner or later recognize and accept the necessity of expressing themselves with utmost sincerity. I am rather referring to a kind of self-expression which is as little at the patient's conscious command as it is at the composer's command to express his feelings in music. If factors within himself bar him from expression, the composer is flatly unable to work; he is unproductive.

Similarly, a patient, despite his best intentions to be co-operative, becomes unproductive as soon as his efforts meet some "resistance." But the more frequent the periods in which he is able to express himself freely, the more he can tackle his own problems and the more significant is the common work of patient and analyst.

I have often told my patients that it would be ideal if the analyst merely played the part of a guide on a difficult mountain tour, indicating which way would be profitable to take or to avoid. To be accurate one should add that the analyst is a guide who is not too certain of the way himself, because though experienced in mountain climbing he has not yet climbed this particular mountain. And this fact makes the patient's mental activity and productivity all the more desirable. It is scarcely an overstatement that, apart from the analyst's competence, it is the patient's constructive activity that determines the length and outcome of an analysis.

The significance of the patient's mental activity in analytical therapy is often revealed when an analysis has to be interrupted or terminated for some reason or other while the patient is still in a bad condition. Both patient and analyst are dissatisfied with the progress attained, but after some time has elapsed without further analysis, they may find themselves pleasantly surprised by the patient's considerable and lasting improvement. If careful examination does not show any change in his circumstances that might account for the improvement, one may be justified in regarding it as a belated effect of analysis. Such an aftereffect, however, is not easy to ac-

14

count for. Various factors may contribute to it. The previous work may have enabled the patient to make such accurate self-observations that he is convinced more deeply than before of the existence of certain disturbing trends, or is even able to discover new factors within himself. Or it may be that he had regarded any suggestion made by the analyst as a foreign intrusion and that he can take hold of insights more easily when they re-emerge as his own findings. Or, if his trouble was a rigid need to be superior to others and to defeat them, he may have been incapable of giving the analyst the satisfaction of doing successful work, and thus be able to recover only when the analyst is out of the picture. Finally, it must be remembered that delayed reactions occur also in many other situations: only much later may we grasp the real meaning of a joke or a remark made in a conversation.

Different as these explanations are they all point in one direction: they suggest that some mental activity must have gone on in the patient without his being aware of it, or at least without consciously determined efforts. That such mental activities, and even meaningful directed activities, do occur without awareness we know from the existence of meaningful dreams and from such experiences as being balked by a task in the evening and knowing the solution after awakening from sleep. Not only is there the famous mathematical problem, of which the solution presents itself in the morning, but a decision befogged in the evening may be clarified after having "slept" over it. A resentment not even perceived in daytime may have worked itself through to awareness so keenly that we awake suddenly at five o'clock in the morning, clearly recognizing provocation and reaction.

As a matter of fact, every analyst relies on the operation of these underground mental activities. Such reliance is implicit in the doctrine that an analysis will proceed satisfactorily if the "resistances" are removed. I should like to stress also the positive aspect: the stronger and the less hampered a patient's incentive toward liberation, the more productive activity will he display. But whether one emphasize the negative aspect (resistance) or the positive one (incentive), the underlying principle is the same: by removing obstacles or by eliciting sufficient incentive the patient's mental energy will be set to work and he will produce material that will eventually lead to some further insight.

The question raised in this book is whether one could go one step further. If the analyst relies on the patient's unconscious mental activity, if the patient has the faculty to work alone toward the solution of some problem, could this faculty be utilized in a more deliberate fashion? Could the patient scrutinize his self-observations or his associations with his own critical intelligence? Usually there is a division of labor between patient and analyst. By and large, the patient lets his thoughts, feelings, and impulses emerge, and the analyst uses his critical intelligence to recognize what the patient is driving at. He questions the validity of statements, he puts together seemingly disconnected material, he makes suggestions as to possible meanings. I said "by and large" because the analyst uses also his intuition and the patient, too, may tie things together. But on the whole such a division of labor exists, and it has definite advantages for the analytical session. It enables the patient to relax and merely express or register whatever emerges.

But what about the day or the days between the analytical sessions? What about longer interruptions that occur for various reasons? Why leave it to accident that some problem will inadvertently clarify itself? Would it not be possible to encourage the patient not only to make deliberate and accurate self-observations but also to arrive at some insight by using his power of reasoning? Granted it would be a hard job fraught with hazards and limitations—which will be discussed later—these difficulties should not prevent us from raising the question: is it impossible to analyze oneself?

In a broader frame of reference this question is one of venerable age: can one recognize oneself? It is encouraging to find that people have always regarded this task, though difficult, as feasible. The encouragement, however, does not carry us far, because there is a vast distance between the way the ancients looked at this task and the way we look at it. We know, particularly since Freud's basic findings, that the task is infinitely more intricate and difficult than the ancients ever imagined—so difficult, indeed, that it is like an adventure into the unknown merely to raise the question seriously.

In recent times any number of books have appeared with the purpose of helping people to cope better with themselves and others. Some of these, like Dale Carnegie's *How to Win Friends and Influence People,* have little if anything to do with recognition of self but offer rather more or less good common-sense advice on how to deal with personal and social problems. But some, like David Seabury's *Adventures in Self-Discovery,* definitely aim at self-analysis. If I feel the need to write another book on the subject it is because I believe that even the best of these authors, such as Seabury, do not make sufficient use of the psychoanalytical technique inaugurated by Freud and hence give insufficient instruction.* Furthermore, they do not recognize the intricacies involved, as appears clearly in such titles as *Self-Analysis Made Easy.* The tendency expressed in books of this kind is implicit also in certain psychiatric attempts at personality studies.

All these attempts suggest that it is an easy matter to recognize oneself. This is an illusion, a belief built on wishful thinking, and a positively harmful illusion at that. People who embark on that promised easy road will either acquire a false smugness, believing they know all about themselves, or will become discouraged when they are blocked by the first serious obstacle and will tend to relinquish the search for truth as a bad job. Neither result will happen so easily if one is aware that self-analysis is a strenuous, slow process, bound to be painful and

* Harold D. Lasswell in Chapter 4, "Know Thyself," in his *Democracy Through Public Opinion,* points out the value of free association for self-recognition. But since the book is devoted to another subject he does not discuss the specific issues involved in the question of self-analysis.

upsetting at times and requiring all available constructive energies.

An experienced analyst would never succumb to such optimism because he is too familiar with the hard and sometimes desperate fight that a patient may put up before he is capable of facing a problem squarely. An analyst would rather tend toward the opposite extreme of rejecting the possibility of self-analysis altogether, and he would be so inclined not only because of his experience but also on theoretical grounds. He would bring forth the argument, for instance, that a patient can free himself from his difficulties only when re-experiencing his infantile desires, fears, and attachments in relation to the analyst; left to his own devices the patient could at best reach ineffective, "merely intellectual" insights. If arguments such as this were scrutinized in detail—which will not be done here—they would ultimately boil down to a disbelief that the patient's incentive is strong enough to enable him to overcome by himself the obstacles littering the road to self-recognition.

I am stressing this point for good reasons. The patient's incentive to arrive at some goal is an important factor in every analysis. One may safely say that an analyst cannot bring the patient any further than the patient himself wants to go. In an analysis, however, the patient has the advantage of the analyst's help, his encouragement, his guidance, the value of which we shall discuss in another chapter. If the patient is left to his own resources the matter of incentive becomes crucial—so crucial, indeed, that the feasibility of self-analysis hinges on its strength.

Freud, of course, recognized that manifest gross suffering under neurotic problems may provide such an incentive. But apparently he felt at a loss to account for an incentive if gross suffering has never existed or has disappeared during treatment. He suggested that the patient's "love" for the analyst might provide an additional incentive, provided this "love" does not aim at a concrete sexual satisfaction but is contented with receiving and utilizing the analyst's help. This sounds plausible. We must not forget, however, that in every neurosis the ability to love is greatly impaired, and that what appears as such is mostly the result of the patient's excessive need for affection and approval. It is true that there are patients—and I suppose Freud had them in mind—who go to considerable lengths to please the analyst, including a willingness to accept interpretations more or less uncritically and including also an attempt to show improvement. Efforts of this type, however, are not prompted by "love" for the analyst, but represent the patient's means of allaying his lurking fear of people and in a broader sense his way of coping with life, for he feels helpless to do it in a more self-reliant manner. In consequence, this motivation to do good work depends entirely on the relationship with the analyst. As soon as the patient feels rejected or criticized—as this type does easily—he will lose sight of his own interest, and the psychoanalytical work then becomes the battlefield for the patient's spite and vengeance. Almost more important than the unreliability of this incentive: the analyst has to discourage it. The tendency to do things merely because someone else expects it, regardless of his own wishes, is a considerable source of trouble to the patient; therefore it has to be analyzed, not utilized. Thus the only effective incentive that Freud recognized remains the patient's wish to get rid of manifest gross suffering; and this motivation, as Freud rightly asserted, does not carry far because it is bound to diminish in exact proportion with a decrease of symptoms.

Still, this incentive might suffice if a removal of symptoms were the only goal of analysis. But is it? Freud never expressed unambiguously his view of these goals. To say that a patient should become capable of work and enjoyment is not meaningful without a qualification of both capacities. Capable of routine work or of creative work? Capable of enjoying sexuality or life in general? To say that analysis should constitute a re-education is likewise vague without an answer to the question, education for what? Probably Freud did not give this question much thought because from his earliest to his latest writings he was primarily interested in the removal of neurotic symptoms; he cared about a change of personality only in so far as it would guarantee a permanent cure of symptoms.

Freud's goal is thus essentially to be defined in a negative manner: gaining "freedom from." Other authors, however, including myself, would formulate the goal of analysis in a positive way: by rendering a person free from inner bondages make him free for the development of his best potentialities. This may sound like a mere difference in emphasis, but, even if it were nothing but that, the different emphasis suffices to alter the matter of incentive entirely.

To set the goal in the positive fashion has a realistic value only if there is in the patient an incentive, sufficiently powerful to be reckoned with, to develop whatever faculties he has, to realize given potentialities, to come to grips with himself despite all the ordeals he may have to go through at times; to put it in the simplest way possible, if there is an incentive to grow.

When the issue is stated thus plainly it is clear that there is more involved here than a difference in emphasis, because Freud emphatically denied that such a wish exists. He even scoffed at it, as if the positing of such a wish were a sort of hollow idealism. He pointed out that urges toward self-development emanate from "narcissistic" desires, that is, they represent a tendency toward self-inflation and toward excelling others. Freud rarely made a postulate merely for the love of theoretical considerations. At bottom there was almost always some astute observation. In this instance it is the observation that tendencies toward self-aggrandizement are sometimes a forceful element in the wish for self-development. What Freud refused to recognize is the fact that this "narcissistic" element is a contributing factor only. If the need for self-aggrandizement has been analyzed and abandoned, the wish to develop still remains, yes, it emerges more clearly and powerfully than before. The "narcissistic" elements, while they have kindled the wish

22

to grow, have at the same time hampered its realization. To use the words of a patient: "The 'narcissistic' impulse is toward the development of a phony self." The fostering of this phony self is always at the expense of the real self, the latter being treated with disdain, at best like a poor relation. My experience is that the more the phony self evaporates, the more the real self becomes invested with interest and the more unbridled an incentive emerges to unfold by becoming free from internal bondages, to live as full a life as given circumstances permit. It seems to me that the wish for developing one's energies belongs among those strivings that defy further analysis.

Theoretically, Freud's disbelief in a wish for self-development is linked up with his postulate that the "ego" is a weak agency tossed about among the claims of instinctual drives, of the outside world and of a forbidding conscience. Ultimately, however, I believe that the two formulations of analytical goals are expressions of different philosophical beliefs as to the nature of man. In the words of Max Otto: "The deepest source of a man's philosophy, the one that shapes and nourishes it, is faith or lack of faith in mankind. If he has confidence in human beings and believes that something fine can be achieved through them, he will acquire ideas about life and about the world which are in harmony with his confidence. Lack of confidence will generate corresponding ideas." It may be mentioned that Freud, in his book on the interpretation of dreams, at least implicitly recognized that some degree of self-analysis is possible, for here he did analyze his own dreams. This is particularly interesting in view of the fact that his whole philosophy denied the possibility of self-analysis.

But even if we grant that there is sufficient incentive for self-analysis there is still the question whether it can be undertaken by a "layman" who has not the necessary knowledge, training, and experience. It may well be asked, and with some asperity, whether I am suggesting that three or four chapters of this book can constitute an adequate substitute for the specific skills of an expert. Naturally, I do not hold any substitute to be possible. I do not aspire to offer even an approximate substitute. Thus it appears that here we are at an impasse. But are we really? Usually the application of an all-or-nothing principle implies some fallacy despite apparent plausibility. In regard to this problem it is desirable to remember, with all due respect for the role of specialization in cultural development, that too much awe of specialization can paralyze initiative. We are all too inclined to believe that only a politician can understand politics, that only a mechanic can repair our car, that only a trained gardener can prune our trees. Of course, a trained person can perform more quickly and more efficiently than an untrained person, and in many instances the latter will fail entirely. But the gap between a trained and an untrained person is often regarded as wider than it is. Faith in specialization can easily turn into blind awe and stifle any attempt at new activity.

General considerations of this kind are encouraging. But in order to arrive at a proper evaluation of the technical possibility of self-analysis we must visualize in concrete detail what constitutes the equipment of a professional analyst. In the first place, the analysis of others demands an extensive psychological knowledge of the nature of unconscious forces, the forms of their manifestation, the reasons responsible for their power, the influence wielded by them, the ways of unearthing them. In the second place, it demands definite skills, which must be developed by training and experience: the analyst must understand how to deal with the patient; he must know with a reasonable degree of certainty which factors in the maze of material presented should be tackled and which left out for the time being; he must have acquired a highly developed ability to "feel into" the patient, a sensitivity to psychic undercurrents that is almost a sixth sense. Finally, the analysis of others demands a thorough self-knowledge. In working with a patient the analyst has to project himself into a strange world, with its own peculiarities and its own laws. And there is considerable danger that he will misconstrue, mislead, perhaps even inflict positive injury—not through bad will but through carelessness, ignorance, or conceit. Therefore not only must he have a thorough familiarity with his tools, and skill in using them, but, equally important, he must be straightened out in his relations to self and others. Since all three of these requirements are indispensable, nobody who does not fulfill them should assume the responsibility involved in analyzing others.

These requirements cannot be automatically attributed to self-analysis as well, because analyzing ourselves is in certain essential points different from analyzing others. The difference most pertinent here is the fact that the world that each of us represents is not strange to ourselves; it is, in fact, the only one we really know. True enough, a neurotic person has become estranged from large parts of this world and has an impelling interest not to see parts of it. Also there is always the danger that in his familiarity with himself he will take certain significant factors too much for granted. But the fact remains that it is his world, that all the knowledge about it is there somehow, that he need only observe and make use of his observations in order to gain access to it. If he is interested in recognizing the sources of his difficulties, if he can overcome his resistances to recognizing them, he can in some respects observe himself better than an outsider can. After all, he lives with himself day and night. In his chances to make self-observations he might be compared with an intelligent nurse who is constantly with a patient; an analyst, however, sees the patient at best only for an hour each day. The analyst has better methods for observation, and clearer viewpoints from which to observe and to make inferences, but the nurse has opportunities for a wider range of observation.

This fact constitutes an important asset in self-analysis. Indeed, it reduces the first of the requirements demanded of a professional analyst and eliminates the second: in self-analysis less psychological knowledge is demanded than in the analysis of others, and we do not need at all the strategical skill that is necessary in dealing with any other person. The crucial difficulty in self-analysis lies not in these fields but in the emotional factors that blind us to unconscious forces. That the main difficulty is emotional rather than intellectual is confirmed by the fact that when analysts analyze themselves they have not such a great advantage over the layman as we would be inclined to believe.

On theoretical grounds, then, I see no stringent reason why self-analysis should not be feasible. Granted that many people are too deeply entangled in their own problems to be able to analyze themselves; granted that self-analysis can never approximate the speed and accuracy of analytical treatment by an expert; granted that there are certain resistances that can be surmounted only with outside help—still, all of this is no proof that in principle the job cannot be done.

I should not dare, however, to raise the question of self-analysis on the basis of theoretical considerations alone. The courage to raise the question, and to do it seriously, has arisen from experiences indicating that self-analysis is possible. These are experiences that I have had myself, that colleagues have had and told me about, that patients have had whom I have encouraged to work on themselves during interruptions of the analytical work with me. These successful attempts did not concern merely superficial difficulties. In fact, some of them dealt with problems that are generally deemed inaccessible even with the help of an analyst. They were made, however, under one favorable condition: all of these people had been analyzed before they ventured on

27

self-analysis, which means that they were familiar with the method of approach and knew from experience that in analysis nothing short of ruthless honesty with oneself is helpful. Whether and to what extent self-analysis is possible without such previous experience must be left an open question. There is, however, the encouraging fact that many people gain an accurate insight into their problems before coming for treatment. These insights are insufficient, to be sure, but the fact remains that they were acquired without previous analytical experience.

Thus the possibilities of self-analysis are briefly as follows, provided a person is capable at all of analyzing himself, of which something will be said later. A patient may undertake it during the longer intervals that occur in most analyses: holidays, absences from the city, for professional or personal reasons, various other interruptions. A person who lives outside the few cities in which there are competent analysts may attempt to carry the main work by himself and see an analyst only for occasional checkups; the same would hold for those who live in a city in which there are analysts but for financial reasons cannot afford regular treatments. And it may be possible for a person whose analysis has been prematurely ended to carry on by himself. Finally—and this with a question mark—self-analysis may be feasible without outside analytical help.

But here is another question. Granted that within limitations it is possible to analyze oneself, is it desirable?

28

Is not analysis too dangerous a tool to use without the guidance of a competent person? Did not Freud compare analysis with surgery—though adding that people do not die because of a wrong application of analysis as they might from an operation badly handled?

Since it is never constructive to remain in the limbo of vague apprehensions, let us try to examine in detail what the possible dangers of self-analysis may be. In the first place, many people will think that it might increase unwholesome introspection. The same objection has been raised, and is still being raised, against any type of analysis, but I should like to reopen this discussion because I am certain that it will be waged even more loudly if analysis is conducted without, or with little, guidance.

The disapproval expressed in the apprehension that analysis might render a person more introspective seems to arise from a philosophy of life—well represented in *The Late George Apley*—which grants no place to the individual or his individual feelings and strivings. What counts is that he fit into the environment, be of service to the community, and fulfill his duties. Hence whatever individual fears or desires he has should be controlled. Self-discipline is the uppermost virtue. To give much thought to himself in any way is self-indulgence and "selfishness." The best representatives of psychoanalysis, on the other hand, would emphasize not only the responsibility toward others but that toward oneself as well. Therefore they would not neglect to stress the inalienable right of the individual to the pursuit of happiness,

29

including his right to take seriously his development toward inner freedom and autonomy.

Each individual must make his own decision as to the value of the two philosophies. If he decides for the former there is not much sense in arguing with him about analysis, because he is bound to feel it not right that anyone should give so much thought to himself and his problems. One can merely reassure him that as a result of analysis the individual usually becomes less egocentric and more reliable in his human relationships; then at best he might concede that introspection may be a debatable means to a worthy end.

A person whose beliefs conform with the other philosophy could not possibly hold that introspection in itself is blameworthy. For him the recognition of self is as important as the recognition of other factors in the environment; to search for truth about self is as valuable as to search for truth in other areas of life. The only question that would concern him is whether introspection is constructive or futile. I would say that it is constructive if it is used in the service of a wish to become a better, richer, and stronger human being—if it is a responsible endeavor of which the ultimate goal is self-recognition and change. If it is an end in itself, that is, if it is pursued merely out of indiscriminate interest in psychological connections—art for art's sake—then it can easily degenerate into what Houston Peterson calls "mania psychologica." And it is equally futile if it consists merely of immersion in self-admiration or self-pity, dead-end ruminations about oneself, empty self-recrimination.

30

And here we arrive at the pertinent point: would not self-analysis easily degenerate into just that type of aimless pondering? Judging from my experience with patients, I believe that this danger is not so general as one might be inclined to think. It appears safe to assume that only those would succumb to it who tend also in their work with an analyst to move constantly in blind alleys of this kind. Without guidance these persons would become lost in futile wanderings. But even so, their attempts at self-analysis, while doomed to failure, could scarcely be harmful, because it is not the analysis that causes their ruminations. They pondered about their bellyache or their appearance, about wrong done by them or to them, or spun out elaborate and aimless "psychological explanations" before they ever came in touch with analysis. By them analysis is used—or abused—as justification for continuing to move in their old circles: it provides the illusion that the circular movements are honest self-scrutiny. We should therefore reckon these attempts among the limitations rather than among the dangers of self-analysis.

In considering the possible dangers of self-analysis the essential problem is whether it involves a risk of definite harm to the individual. By endeavoring on this adventure singlehanded does he not conjure up hidden forces with which he is unable to cope? If he recognizes a crucial unconscious conflict, without yet seeing a way out, are there not aroused in him such deep feelings of anxiety and helplessness that he might succumb to a depression, or even consider suicide?

We must distinguish in this regard between transitory and lasting impairments. Transitory impairments are bound to occur in every analysis, because any reaching down to repressed material must stir up anxiety previously allayed by defensive measures. Likewise, it must bring to the foreground affects of anger and rage otherwise shut off from awareness. This shock effect is so strong not because the analysis has led to the recognition of some intolerably bad or vicious trend, but because it has shaken an equilibrium which, though precarious, had prevented the individual from feeling lost in the chaos of diverging drives. Since we shall discuss later the nature of these transitory disturbances, it may suffice here to state merely the fact that they occur.

When a patient meets such a disturbance during the analytical process he may simply feel profoundly perturbed or he may have recurrences of old symptoms. Naturally, then, he feels discouraged. These setbacks are usually overcome after a short while. As soon as the new insight is really integrated they vanish and give way to the well-founded feeling of having taken a step ahead. They represent the shocks and pains unavoidably involved in a reorientation of life, and are implicit in any constructive process.

It is at these periods of inner upheaval that the patient would particularly miss the helping hand of an analyst. But we are taking it for granted that the whole process is easier with competent help. Here we are concerned with the possibility that the individual might not be able to overcome these upsets alone and thus be permanently impaired. Or that when he feels his foundations shaken he might do something desperate, such as driving or gambling recklessly, jeopardizing his position, or attempting suicide.

In the cases of self-analysis which I have observed such untoward consequences have never occurred. But these observations are as yet too limited to produce any convincing statistical evidence; I could not say, for instance, that this unfortunate outcome has occurred in only one case out of a hundred. There are, however, good reasons to believe that the danger is so rare as to be negligible. Observation in every analysis shows that patients are well able to protect themselves from insights they are not yet able to receive. If they are given an interpretation that represents too great a threat to their security they may consciously reject it; or they may forget it, or invalidate its relevance for them, or ward it off with arguments, or simply resent it as unfair criticism.

One may safely assume that these self-protective forces would operate also in self-analysis. A person attempting to analyze himself would simply fail to make any self-observations that would lead to insights as yet intolerable. Or he would interpret them in such a way as to miss the essential point. Or he would merely try to correct quickly and superficially an attitude conceived by him as faulty, and thereby close the door to further investigation. Thus in self-analysis the actual danger would be less than in professional analysis, because the patient intuitively knows what to avoid while an analyst, even a sensitive one, may err and present to the patient a pre-

33

mature solution. Again the danger is one of futility through too much evasion of problems rather than of positive damage.

And if a person does work through to some insight deeply disturbing to him, I believe there are several considerations that we can rely upon. One is that hitting upon some truth is not only disturbing but is also, and simultaneously, of a liberating quality. This liberating force inherent in any truth may supersede the disturbing effect from the beginning. If so, a feeling of relief will ensue immediately. But even if the disturbing effect prevails, the discovery of a truth about oneself still implies a dawning recognition of a way out; even if this is not seen clearly it will be felt intuitively and thus will engender strength to proceed further.

A second factor to be considered is that even if a truth is deeply frightening there is something like a wholesome fright. If a person recognizes, for instance, that he has been secretly driving at self-destruction, his clear recognition of that drive is much less dangerous than letting it silently operate. The recognition is frightening, but it is bound to mobilize counteracting self-preserving energies, provided there is any will to live. And if there is no sufficient will to live, a person will go to pieces anyhow, analysis or no analysis. To express a similar thought in a more positive fashion: if a person has had sufficient courage to discover an unpleasant truth about himself, one may safely trust his courage to be strong enough to carry him through. The mere fact that he has gone that far indicates that his will to come to grips with himself

34

is strong enough to prevent him from becoming crushed. But the period between starting to grapple with a problem and solving and integrating it may be prolonged in self-analysis.

Finally, we must not forget that really alarming disturbances in analysis rarely occur only because an interpretation cannot be properly grasped at the time. More frequently the real source of disquieting developments lies in the fact that the interpretation, or the analytical situation as a whole, stirs up hatred that is directed against the analyst. This hatred, if barred from awareness and thereby from expression, can enhance existing self-destructive tendencies. To let oneself go to pieces may then become a means of revenge against the analyst.

If a person is confronted with an upsetting insight quite by himself, there is almost nothing left but to fight it through with himself. Or, to be cautious, the temptation to ward off the insight by making others responsible is lessened. The caution is warranted because, if the tendency to make others responsible for his shortcomings is strong anyhow, it may flare up also in self-analysis as soon as he realizes a shortcoming, if he has not yet accepted the necessity of taking responsibility for himself.

I would say, then, that self-analysis is within the range of possibility, and that the danger of its resulting in positive damage is comparatively slight. Certainly it has various drawbacks that are more or less serious in nature, ranging, briefly, from failure to prolongation of the process; it may take a considerably longer time to get hold of a problem and to solve it. But against these drawbacks there are many factors which beyond doubt make self-analysis desirable. There are, to begin with, obvious external factors of the kind mentioned before. Self-analysis would be desirable for those who because of money, time, or location cannot undertake regular treatment. And even for those who are having treatment it might shorten the procedure considerably if in the intervals between analytical sessions, and also during the sessions, they were inspired with the courage to do active and independent work on themselves.

But even apart from such blatant reasons, certain gains are beckoning to those who are capable of self-analysis which are more spiritual in character, less tangible but not less real. These gains can be summarized as an increase of inner strength and therefore of self-confidence. Every successful analysis increases self-confidence, but there is a certain extra gain in having conquered territory entirely through one's own initiative, courage, and perseverance. This effect is the same in analysis as in other areas of life. To find a mountain path all by oneself gives a greater feeling of strength than to take a path that is shown, though the work put in is the same and the result is the same. Such achievement gives rise not only to a justifiable pride but also to a well-founded feeling of confidence in one's capacity to meet predicaments and not to feel lost without guidance.

36

CHAPTER TWO

The Driving Forces in Neuroses

Psychoanalysis, as already discussed, has not only a clinical value as a therapy for neuroses but also a human value in its potentialities for helping people toward their best possible further development. Both objectives can be pursued in other ways; peculiar to analysis is the attempt to reach these goals through human understanding—not alone through sympathy, tolerance, and an intuitive grasp of interconnections, qualities that are indispensable in any kind of human understanding, but, more fundamentally, through an effort to obtain an accurate picture of the total personality. This is undertaken by means of specific techniques for unearthing unconscious factors, for Freud has clearly shown that we cannot obtain such a picture without recognizing the role of unconscious forces. Through him we know that such forces push us into actions and feelings and responses that may be different from what we consciously desire and may even be destructive of satisfactory relations with the world around us.

Certainly these unconscious motivations exist in everyone, and are by no means always productive of disturbances. It is only when disturbances exist that it is important to uncover and recognize the unconscious factors. No matter what unconscious forces drive us to paint or to write, we would scarcely bother to think about them if we can express ourselves in painting or writing with reasonable adequacy. No matter what unconscious motivations carry us away to love or devotion, we are not interested in them so long as that love or devotion gives a constructive content to our lives. But we do need to consider the unconscious factors if apparent success in doing productive work or in establishing a good human relationship, a success that we desperately wanted, leaves us only empty and disgruntled, or if one attempt after another fails and, despite all efforts to the contrary, we feel dimly that we cannot put the failures altogether on external circumstances. In short, we need to examine our unconscious motivations if it appears that something from within is hampering us in our pursuits.

Since Freud unconscious motivations have been accepted as elemental facts of human psychology, and the subject need not be elaborated here, especially since everyone can enlarge his knowledge about unconscious motivations in various ways. There are, in the first place, Freud's own writings, such as his *Introductory Lectures*

38

on *Psychoanalysis, Psychopathology of Everyday Life,* and *The Interpretation of Dreams,* and the books summarizing his theories, such as Ives Hendrick's *Facts and Theories of Psychoanalysis.* Also worth consulting are those authors who try to develop Freud's basic findings, such as H. S. Sullivan in his *Conceptions of Modern Psychiatry,* Edward A. Strecker in *Beyond the Clinical Frontiers,* Erich Fromm in *Escape from Freedom,* or myself in *The Neurotic Personality of Our Time* and in *New Ways in Psychoanalysis.* A. H. Maslow and Bela Mittelmann in *Principles of Abnormal Psychology,* and Fritz Kunkel's books, such as *Character Growth and Education,* suggest many valuable leads. Philosophical books, particularly the writings of Emerson, Nietzsche, and Schopenhauer, reveal psychological treasures for those who read them with an open mind, as do a few of the books on the art of living, such as Charles Allen Smart's *Wild Geese and How to Chase Them.* Shakespeare, Balzac, Dostoevski, Ibsen, and others are inexhaustible sources of psychological knowledge. And by no means least, a lot can be learned from observing the world around us.

A knowledge of the existence and efficacy of such unconscious motivations is a helpful guide in any attempt at analysis, particularly if it is not merely given lip service but is taken seriously. It may even be a sufficient tool for sporadically discovering this or that causal connection. For a more systematic analysis, however, it is necessary to have a somewhat more specific understanding of the unconscious factors that disturb development.

39

In any effort to understand personality it is essential to discover the underlying driving forces of that personality. In attempting to understand a disturbed personality it is essential to discover the driving forces responsible for the disturbance.

Here we are on more controversial ground. Freud believed that the disturbances generate from a conflict between environmental factors and repressed instinctual impulses. Adler, more rationalistic and superficial than Freud, believes that they are created by the ways and means that people use to assert their superiority over others. Jung, more mystical than Freud, believes in collective unconscious fantasies which, though replete with creative possibilities, may work havoc because the unconscious strivings fed by them are the exact opposite of those in the conscious mind. My own answer is that in the center of psychic disturbances are unconscious strivings developed in order to cope with life despite fears, helplessness, and isolation. I have called them "neurotic trends." My answer is as far from final as that of Freud or Jung. But every explorer into the unknown has some vision of what he expects to find, and he can have no guarantee of the correctness of his vision. Discoveries have been made even though the vision was incorrect. This fact may serve as a consolation for the uncertainty of our present psychological knowledge.

What then are neurotic trends? What are their characteristics, their function, their genesis, their effect on one's life? It should be emphasized again that their essen-

tial elements are unconscious. A person may be aware of
their effects, though in that case he will probably merely
credit himself with laudable character traits: if he has,
for example, a neurotic need for affection he will think
that his is a good and loving disposition; or if he is in
the grip of a neurotic perfectionism he will think that
he is by nature more orderly and accurate than others.
He may even glimpse something of the drives producing
such effects, or recognize them when they are brought
to his attention: he may become aware, for example, that
he has a need for affection or a need to be perfect. But
he is never aware to what extent he is in the grip of these
strivings, to what extent they determine his life. Still less
is he aware of the reasons why they have such power over
him.

The outstanding characteristic of neurotic trends is
their compulsive nature, a quality that shows itself in
two main ways. First, their objectives are pursued indis-
criminately. If it is affection a person must have, he must
receive it from friend and enemy, from employer and
bootblack. A person obsessed by a need for perfection
largely loses his sense of proportion. To have his desk in
faultless order becomes as imperative for him as to prepare an important report in perfect fashion. Moreover,
the objectives are pursued with supreme disregard for
reality and real self-interest. A woman hanging on to a
man to whom she relegates all responsibility for her life
may be utterly oblivious to such questions as whether
that particular man is an entirely appropriate person to
hang on to, whether she is actually happy with him,

41

whether she likes and respects him. If a person must be independent and self-sufficient he will refuse to tie himself to anyone or anything, no matter how much he spoils his life thereby; he must not ask or accept help, no matter how much he needs it. This absence of discrimination is often obvious to others, but the person himself may not be aware of it. As a rule, however, it will strike the outsider only if the particular trends are inconvenient to him or if they do not coincide with recognized patterns. He will notice, for instance, a compulsive negativism but may not become aware of a compulsive compliance.

The second indication of the compulsive nature of neurotic trends is the reaction of anxiety that ensues from their frustration. This characteristic is highly significant, because it demonstrates the safety value of the trends. A person feels vitally threatened if for any reason, internal or external, the compulsive pursuits are ineffective. A perfectionistic person feels panicky if he makes any mistake. A person with a compulsive need for unlimited freedom becomes frightened at the prospect of any tie, whether it be an engagement to marry or the lease of an apartment. A good illustration of fear reactions of this kind is contained in Balzac's *Chagrin Leather*. The hero in the novel is convinced that his span of life is shortened whenever he expresses a wish, and therefore he anxiously refrains from doing so. But once, when off his guard, he does express a wish, and even though the wish itself is unimportant he becomes panicky. The example illustrates the terror that seizes a neurotic person if his security is threatened: he feels that everything is lost if he lapses from perfection, complete independence, or whatever standard it is that represents his driving need. It is this security value that is primarily responsible for the compulsive character of the neurotic trends.

The function of these trends can be better understood if we take a look at their genesis. They develop early in life through the combined effect of given temperamental and environmental influences. Whether a child becomes submissive or rebellious under the pressure of parental coercion depends not only on the nature of the coercion but also on given qualities, such as the degree of his vitality, the relative softness or hardness of his nature. Since we know less of the constitutional factors than of the environmental ones, and since the latter are the only ones susceptible of change, I shall comment only on these.

Under all conditions a child will be influenced by his environment. What counts is whether this influence stunts or furthers growth. And which development will occur depends largely on the kind of relationship established between the child and his parents or others around him, including other children in the family. If the spirit at home is one of warmth, of mutual respect and consideration, the child can grow unimpeded.

Unfortunately, in our civilization there are many environmental factors adverse to a child's development. Parents, with the best of intentions, may exert so much pressure on the child that his initiative becomes paralyzed. There may be a combination of smothering love and intimidation, of tyranny and glorification. Parents may impress the child with the dangers awaiting him outside the walls of his home. One parent may force the child to side with him against the other. Parents may be unpredictable and sway from a jolly comradeship to a strict authoritarianism. Particularly important, a child may be led to feel that his right to existence lies solely in his living up to the parents' expectations—measuring up to their standards or ambitions for him, enhancing their prestige, giving them blind devotion; in other words, he may be prevented from realizing that he is an individual with his own rights and his own responsibilities. The effectiveness of such influences is not diminished by the fact that they are often subtle and veiled. Moreover, there is usually not just one adverse factor but several in combination.

As a consequence of such an environment the child does not develop a proper self-respect. He becomes insecure, apprehensive, isolated, and resentful. At the beginning he is helpless toward these forces around him, but gradually, by intuition and experience, he develops means of coping with the environment and of saving his own skin. He develops a wary sensitivity as to how to manipulate others.

The particular techniques that he develops depend on the whole constellation of circumstances. One child realizes that by stubborn negativism and occasional temper tantrums he can ward off intrusion. He shuts others out of his life, living on a private island of which he is master and resenting every demand made upon him, every suggestion or expectation, as a dangerous inroad on his privacy. For another child no other way is open than to eradicate himself and his feelings and submit blindly, eking out merely a little spot here and there where he is free to be himself. These unoccupied territories may be primitive or sublime. They range from secret masturbation in the seclusion of the bathroom to the realm of nature, books, fantasies. In contrast to this way, a third child does not freeze his emotions but clings to the most powerful of the parents in a kind of desperate devotion. He blindly adopts that parent's likes and dislikes, his way of living, his philosophy of life. He may suffer under this tendency, however, and develop simultaneously a passionate desire for self-sufficiency.

Thus the foundations are laid for the neurotic trends. They represent a way of life enforced by unfavorable conditions. The child must develop them in order to survive his insecurity, his fears, his loneliness. But they give him an unconscious feeling that he must stick to the established path at all odds, lest he succumb to the dangers threatening him.

I believe that with sufficient detailed knowledge of relevant factors in childhood, one can understand why a child develops a particular set of trends. It is not possible here to substantiate this assertion, because to do so would necessitate recording a number of child histories in great detail. But it is not necessary to substantiate it, because everyone sufficiently experienced with children or with reconstructing their early development can test it out for himself.

When this initial development has once occurred is it necessarily lasting? If given circumstances have made a child compliant, defiant, diffident, must he necessarily remain so? The answer is that although he will not inevitably retain his defensive techniques there is grave danger that he will. They can be eradicated by an early radical change of environment, or they can be modified, even after a considerable lapse of time, through any number of fortuitous happenings, such as finding an understanding teacher, a friend, lover, mate, an engrossing task suited to his personality and abilities. But in the absence of strong counteracting factors there is considerable danger that the trends acquired not only will persist but in time will obtain a stronger hold on the personality.

To understand this persistence one must fully realize that these trends are more than a mere strategy evolved as an effective defense against a difficult parent. They are, in view of all the factors developing within, the only possible way for the child to deal with life in general. To run away from attacks is the hare's strategy in the face of dangers, and it is the only strategy he has; he could not possibly decide to fight instead, because he simply has not the means to do so. Similarly, a child growing up under difficult conditions develops a set of attitudes toward life which are fundamentally neurotic trends,

46

Rigidity

and these he cannot change by free will but has to adhere to by necessity. The analogy with the hare is not entirely valid, however, because the hare, by constitution, has no other ways of coping with danger while the human being, if not mentally or physically defective by nature, has other potentialities. His necessity to cling to his special attitudes lies not in constitutional limitations but in the fact that the sum total of his fears, inhibitions, vulnerabilities, false goals, and illusory beliefs about the world confines him to certain ways and excludes others; in other words, it makes him rigid and does not permit of basic alterations.

One way of illustrating this point is to compare how a child and a mature adult may cope with persons presenting comparable difficulties. It must be borne in mind that the following comparison has merely an illustrative value and is not intended to deal with all the factors involved in the two situations. The child, Clare—and here I am thinking of an actual patient to whose analysis I shall return later on—has a self-righteous mother who expects the child's admiration and exclusive devotion. The adult is an employee, psychologically well integrated, who has a boss with qualities similar to those of the mother. Both mother and boss are complacently self-admiring, are arbitrary, favor others unfairly and tend to become hostile if what they regard as due homage is not paid them or if they sense a critical attitude.

Under these conditions the employee, if he has stringent reasons for holding on to his job, will more or less consciously evolve a technique for handling the boss.

He will probably refrain from expressing criticism; make it a point to appreciate explicitly whatever good qualities there are; withhold praise of the boss's competitors; agree with the boss's plans, regardless of his own opinions; let suggestions of his own appear as if the boss had initiated them. And what influence will this strategy have on his personality? He will resent the discrimination and dislike the deceit it necessitates. But since he is a self-respecting person he will feel that the situation reflects on the boss rather than on himself, and the behavior he adopts will not make him a compliant, bootlicking person. His strategy will exist only for that particular boss. Toward the next employer, if a change should take place, he would behave differently.

For an understanding of neurotic trends much depends on recognizing their difference from such *ad hoc* strategy. Otherwise one could not appreciate their force and pervasiveness and would succumb to a mistake similar to Adler's oversimplification and rationality. As a result one would also take too lightly the therapeutic work to be done.

Clare's situation is comparable to that of the employee, for the mother and the boss are similar in character, but for Clare it is worth while to go into more detail. She was an unwanted child. The marriage was unhappy. After having one child, a boy, the mother did not want any more children. Clare was born after several unsuccessful attempts at an abortion. She was not badly treated or neglected in any coarse sense: she was sent to schools as good as those the brother attended, she re-

48

ceived as many gifts as he did, she had music lessons with the same teacher, and in all material ways was treated as well. But in less tangible matters she received less than the brother, less tenderness, less interest in school marks and in the thousand little daily experiences of a child, less concern when she was ill, less solicitude to have her around, less willingness to treat her as a confidante, less admiration for looks and accomplishments. There was a strong, though for a child intangible, community between the mother and brother from which she was excluded. The father was no help. He was absent most of the time, being a country doctor. Clare made some pathetic attempts to get close to him but he was not interested in either of the children. His affection was entirely focused on the mother in a kind of helpless admiration. Finally, he was no help because he was openly despised by the mother, who was sophisticated and attractive and beyond doubt the dominating spirit in the family. The undisguised hatred and contempt the mother felt for the father, including open death wishes against him, contributed much to Clare's feeling that it was much safer to be on the powerful side.

As a consequence of this situation Clare never had a good chance to develop self-confidence. There was not enough of open injustice to provoke sustained rebellion, but she became discontented and cross and complaining. As a result she was teased for always feeling herself a martyr. It never remotely occurred to either mother or brother that she might be right in feeling unfairly treated. They took it for granted that her attitude was a sign of an ugly disposition. And Clare, never having felt secure, easily yielded to the majority opinion about herself and began to feel that everything was her fault. Compared with the mother, whom everyone admired for her beauty and charm, and with the brother, who was cheerful and intelligent, she was an ugly duckling. She became deeply convinced that she was unlikable.

This shift from essentially true and warranted accusations of others to essentially untrue and unwarranted self-accusations had far-reaching consequences, as we shall see presently. And the shift entailed more than an acceptance of the majority estimate of herself. It meant also that she repressed all grievances against the mother. If everything was her own fault the grounds for bearing a grudge against the mother were pulled away from under her. From such repression of hostility it was merely a short step to join the group of those who admired the mother. In this further yielding to majority opinion she had a strong incentive in the mother's antagonism toward everything short of complete admiration: it was much safer to find shortcomings within herself than in the mother. If she, too, admired the mother she need no longer feel isolated and excluded but could hope to receive some affection, or at least be accepted. The hope for affection did not materialize, but she obtained instead a gift of doubtful value. The mother, like all those who thrive on the admiration of others, was generous in giving admiration in turn to those who adored her. Clare was no longer the disregarded ugly duckling, but became the wonderful daughter of a wonderful mother.

Thus, in place of a badly shattered self-confidence, she built up the spurious pride that is founded on outside admiration.

Through this shift from true rebellion to untrue admiration Clare lost the feeble vestiges of self-confidence she had. To use a somewhat vague term, she lost herself. By admiring what in reality she resented, she became alienated from her own feelings. She no longer knew what she herself liked or wished or feared or resented. She lost all capacity to assert her wishes for love, or even any wishes. Despite a superficial pride her conviction of being unlovable was actually deepened. Hence later on, when one or another person was fond of her, she could not take the affection at its face value but discarded it in various ways. Sometimes she would think that such a person misjudged her for something she was not; sometimes she would attribute the affection to gratitude for having been useful or to expectations of her future usefulness. This distrust deeply disturbed every human relationship she entered into. She lost, too, her capacity for critical judgment, acting on the unconscious maxim that it is safer to admire others than to be critical. This attitude shackled her intelligence, which was actually of a high order, and greatly contributed to her feeling stupid.

In consequence of all these factors three neurotic trends developed. One was a compulsive modesty as to her own wishes and demands. This entailed a compulsive tendency to put herself into second place, to think less of herself than of others, to think that others were right and she was wrong. But even in this restricted scope she could not feel safe unless there was someone on whom she could depend, someone who would protect and defend her, advise her, stimulate her, approve of her, be responsible for her, give her everything she needed. She needed all this because she had lost the capacity to take her life into her own hands. Thus she developed the need for a "partner"—friend, lover, husband—on whom she could depend. She would subordinate herself to him as she had toward the mother. But at the same time, by his undivided devotion to her, he would restore her crushed dignity. A third neurotic trend—a compulsive need to excel others and to triumph over them—likewise aimed at restoration of self-regard, but in addition absorbed all the vindictiveness accumulated through hurts and humiliations.

To resume our comparison and summarize what it was meant to illustrate: both the employee and the child develop strategies for dealing with the situation; for both the technique is to put the self into the background and adopt an admiring attitude toward the one in authority. Thus their reactions may appear roughly comparable, but in reality they are entirely different. The employee does not lose his self-regard, does not relinquish his critical judgment, does not repress his resentment. The child, however, loses her self-regard, represses her hostility, abandons her critical faculties and becomes self-effacing. Briefly, the adult merely adjusts his behavior while the child changes her personality.

The inflexible, all-pervasive nature of the neurotic

52

trends has a significant implication for therapy. Patients often expect that as soon as they have detected their compulsive needs they will be able to relinquish them. They are disappointed, then, if the hold these trends have over them persists in scarcely diminished intensity. It is true that these hopes are not entirely fantastic: in mild neuroses the neurotic trend may indeed disappear when it is recognized, as will be discussed in one of the examples cited in the chapter on occasional self-analysis. But in all more intricate neuroses such expectations are as futile as it would be to expect that a social calamity such as unemployment would cease to exist merely because it is recognized as a problem. In each instance, social or personal, it is necessary to study and if possible to influence those forces which have created the disruptive trend and which account for its persistence.

I have emphasized the security offered by the neurotic trends. As mentioned before, this attribute accounts for their compulsive character. But the part played by the feeling of satisfaction that they engender, or the hope for satisfaction, should not be underrated. This feeling or hope is never missing, though its intensity varies. In some neurotic trends, such as the need for perfection or the compulsion toward modesty, the defensive aspect is predominant. In others the satisfaction attained or hoped for through the success of the striving can be so strong that the latter takes on the character of a devouring passion. The neurotic need for dependency, for example, usually entails a vivid expectation of happiness with that person who will take one's life into his hands. A

53

strong tinge of attained or anticipated satisfaction renders a trend less accessible to therapy.

Neurotic trends may be classified in various ways. Those entailing strivings for closeness with others might be contrasted with those aiming at aloofness and distance. Those impelling toward one or another kind of dependency might be bundled together in contrast with those stressing independence. Trends toward expansiveness stand against those working toward a constriction of life. Trends toward an accentuation of personal peculiarities could be contrasted with those aiming at adaptation or at an eradication of the individual self, those toward self-aggrandizement with those that entail self-belittling. But to carry through such classifications would not make the picture clearer, because the categories are overlapping. I shall therefore merely enumerate those trends which at the present time stand out as describable entities. I am positive that the list is neither complete nor clear cut. Other trends will have to be added, and a trend presented as an autonomous entity may turn out to be a mere variety of some other. It would surpass the scope of this chapter to give detailed descriptions of the various trends, even though such knowledge is desirable. Some of them are described in greater detail in previous publications. It must suffice here to list them and to give a cursory enumeration of their main characteristics.

1. The neurotic need for affection and approval (see *The Neurotic Personality of Our Time,* Chapter 6, on the need for affection):

54

Indiscriminate need to please others and to be liked and approved of by others;

Automatic living up to the expectations of others;

Center of gravity in others and not in self, with their wishes and opinions the only thing that counts;

Dread of self-assertion;

Dread of hostility on the part of others or of hostile feelings within self.

2. The neurotic need for a "partner" who will take over one's life (see *New Ways in Psychoanalysis,* Chapter 15, on masochism, and Fromm's *Escape from Freedom,* Chapter 5, on authoritarianism; also the example given below in Chapter 8):

Center of gravity entirely in the "partner," who is to fulfill all expectations of life and take responsibility for good and evil, his successful manipulation becoming the predominant task;

Overevaluation of "love" because "love" is supposed to solve all problems;

Dread of desertion;

Dread of being alone.

3. The neurotic need to restrict one's life within narrow borders:

Necessity to be undemanding and contented with little, and to restrict ambitions and wishes for material things;

Necessity to remain inconspicuous and to take second place;

Belittling of existing faculties and potentialities, with
  modesty the supreme value;
Urge to save rather than to spend;
Dread of making any demands;
Dread of having or asserting expansive wishes.

These three trends are often found together, as might
be expected, because they all entail an admission of
weakness and constitute attempts to arrange life on that
basis. They are the opposite of trends toward relying on
one's own strength or taking responsibility upon oneself. The three of them do not, however, constitute a
syndrome. The third may exist without the other two
playing any noteworthy role.

4. The neurotic need for power (see *The Neurotic
Personality of Our Time*, Chapter 10, on the need for
power, prestige, and possession):
Domination over others craved for its own sake;
Devotion to a cause, duty, responsibility, though play-
  ing some part, not the driving force;
Essential disrespect for others, their individuality, their
  dignity, their feelings, the only concern being their
  subordination;
Great differences as to degree of destructive elements in-
  volved;
Indiscriminate adoration of strength and contempt for
  weakness;
Dread of uncontrollable situations;
Dread of helplessness.

56

4a. The neurotic need to control self and others through reason and foresight (a variety of 4 in people who are too inhibited to exert power directly and openly):

Belief in the omnipotence of intelligence and reason;

Denial of the power of emotional forces and contempt for them;

Extreme value placed on foresight and prediction;

Feelings of superiority over others related to the faculty of foresight;

Contempt for everything within self that lags behind the image of intellectual superiority;

Dread of recognizing objective limitations of the power of reason;

Dread of "stupidity" and bad judgment.

4b. The neurotic need to believe in the omnipotence of will (to use a somewhat ambiguous term, an introvert variety of 4 in highly detached people to whom a direct exertion of power means too much contact with others):

Feeling of fortitude gained from the belief in the magic power of will (like possession of a wishing ring);

Reaction of desolation to any frustration of wishes;

Tendency to relinquish or restrict wishes and to withdraw interest because of a dread of "failure";

Dread of recognizing any limitations of sheer will.

5. The neurotic need to exploit others and by hook or crook get the better of them:

Others evaluated primarily according to whether or not they can be exploited or made use of;

Various foci of exploitation—money (bargaining amounts to a passion), ideas, sexuality, feelings;
Pride in exploitative skill;
Dread of being exploited and thus of being "stupid."

6. The neurotic need for social recognition or prestige (may or may not be combined with a craving for power):
All things—inanimate objects, money, persons, one's own qualities, activities, and feelings—evaluated only according to their prestige value;
Self-evaluation entirely dependent on nature of public acceptance;
Differences as to use of traditional or rebellious ways of inciting envy or admiration;
Dread of losing caste ("humiliation"), whether through external circumstances or through factors from within.

7. The neurotic need for personal admiration:
Inflated image of self (narcissism);
Need to be admired not for what one possesses or presents in the public eye but for the imagined self;
Self-evaluation dependent on living up to this image and on admiration of it by others;
Dread of losing admiration ("humiliation").

8. The neurotic ambition for personal achievement:
Need to surpass others not through what one presents or is but through one's activities;
Self-evaluation dependent on being the very best—lover,

sportsman, writer, worker—particularly in one's own mind, recognition by others being vital too, however, and its absence resented;

Admixture of destructive tendencies (toward the defeat of others) never lacking but varying in intensity;

Relentless driving of self to greater achievements, though with pervasive anxiety;

Dread of failure ("humiliation").

Trends 6, 7, and 8 have in common a more or less open competitive drive toward an absolute superiority over others. But though these trends overlap and may be combined, they may lead a separate existence. The need for personal admiration, for instance, may go with a disregard of social prestige.

9. The neurotic need for self-sufficiency and independence:

Necessity never to need anybody, or to yield to any influence, or to be tied down to anything, any closeness involving the danger of enslavement;

Distance and separateness the only source of security;

Dread of needing others, of ties, of closeness, of love.

10. The neurotic need for perfection and unassailability (see *New Ways in Psychoanalysis,* Chapter 13, on the super-ego, and *Escape from Freedom,* Chapter 5, or automaton conformity):

Relentless driving for perfection;

Ruminations and self-recriminations regarding possible flaws;

Feelings of superiority over others because of being per-
fect;
Dread of finding flaws within self or of making mistakes;
Dread of criticism or reproaches.

A striking consideration in reviewing these trends
is that none of the strivings and attitudes they imply is
in itself "abnormal" or devoid of human value. Most of
us want and appreciate affection, self-control, modesty,
consideration of others. To expect fulfillment of one's
life from another person is regarded, at least for a woman,
as "normal" or even virtuous. Among the strivings are
some that we would not hesitate to estimate highly. Self-
sufficiency, independence, and guidance through reason
are generally regarded as valuable goals.

In view of these facts the question is bound to arise
over and over again: why call these trends neurotic?
What is really wrong with them? Granted that with some
people certain trends are predominant, even have a
measure of rigidity, while quite different trends determine the behavior of others, are not these varieties of
pursuits merely the expression of given differences
among people of different sets of values, different ways
of coping with life? Is it not natural, for instance, that
a tenderhearted person will put stock in affection and a
stronger person in independence and leadership?

To raise these questions is useful because it is not only
of theoretical but of eminently practical importance to
recognize the differences between such basic human
strivings and evaluations and their neurotic counter-

parts. The objectives of the two types of strivings are similar, but their basis and meaning are entirely different. The difference is almost as great as between $+7$ and -7: in both cases we have the number 7, just as we use the same words, affection, reason, perfection, but the prefix changes character and value. The contrasts underlying the apparent similarities have already been touched on in the comparison of the employee and the child Clare, but a few more generalized comparisons may illuminate further the difference between normal and neurotic trends.

A wish for affection from others is meaningful only if there is affection for them, a feeling of having something in common with them. The emphasis then will be not only on the friendliness received but also on the positive feelings one is capable of having for others and of showing to them. But the neurotic need for affection is devoid of the value of reciprocity. For the neurotic person his own feelings of affection count as little as they would if he were surrounded by strange and dangerous animals. To be accurate, he does not even really want the others' affection, but is merely concerned, keenly and strenuously, that they make no aggressive move against him. The singular value lying in mutual understanding, tolerance, concern, sympathy has no place in the relationship.

Similarly, the striving to perfect our gifts and our human faculties is certainly worth our best efforts, so much so that no doubt the world would be a better place to live in if this striving were strong and alive in all of us.

But the neurotic need for perfection, while it may be expressed in identical terms, has lost this special value, because it represents an attempt to be or appear perfect without change. There is no possibility of improvement, because finding areas within the self that would need change is frightening and therefore avoided. The only real concern is to juggle away any deficiency lest one be exposed to attacks, and to preserve the secret feeling of superiority over others. As in the neurotic need for affection, the person's own active participation is lacking or impaired. Instead of being an active striving, this trend is a static insistence upon an illusory *status quo*.

A last comparison: all of us have a high regard for will power, regarding it as a meaningful force if put into the service of pursuits that are themselves important. But the neurotic faith in the omnipotence of will is illusory, because it completely disregards the limitations that may defy even the most determined efforts. No amount of will power gets us out of a Sunday-afternoon traffic jam. Furthermore, the virtue of will power is nullified if the proving of its effectiveness becomes an aim in itself. Any obstacle standing in the way of momentary impulses will drive the person in the grip of this neurotic trend into blind and frantic action, regardless of whether he really wants the particular object. The tables are actually reversed: it is not that he has will power, but that it has him.

These examples may suffice to show that the neurotic pursuits are almost a caricature of the human values they resemble. They lack freedom, spontaneity, and meaning. All too often they involve illusory elements. Their value

62

is only subjective, and lies in the fact that they hold the more or less desperate promise of safety and of a solution for all problems.

And one further point should be emphasized: not only are the neurotic trends devoid of the human values that they mimic, but they do not even represent what the person wants. If he puts all his energies into the pursuit of social prestige or power, for example, he may believe that he really wants these goals; actually, as we have seen, he is merely driven to want them. It is as if he were flying in an airplane which he believes he is piloting, while actually the plane is directed by remote control.

It remains to understand approximately how and to what extent the neurotic trends may determine the person's character and influence his life. In the first place, these pursuits render it necessary for him to develop certain subsidiary attitudes, feelings, and types of behavior. If his trend is toward unlimited independence, he will desire secrecy and seclusion, be wary of anything resembling an intrusion into his privacy, develop techniques for keeping others at a distance. If his trend is toward a constriction of life, he will be modest, undemanding, and ready to yield to anyone who is more aggressive than he.

Also, the neurotic trends largely determine the image a person has of what he is or should be. All neurotic persons are markedly unstable in their self-evaluation, wavering between an inflated and a deflated image of themselves. When a neurotic trend is recognized it becomes possible to understand specifically the reasons why a particular person is aware of certain evaluations of himself and represses others, why he is consciously or unconsciously exceedingly proud of certain attitudes or qualities and despises others for no discernible objective reason.

For example, if A has built up a protective belief in reason and foresight he will not only overrate what can be accomplished by reason in general, but also take a special pride in his power of reasoning, his judgment, his predictions. His notions of his superiority over others will then derive primarily from a conviction that his is a superior intelligence. And if B feels he cannot possibly stand on his own, but must have a "partner" who gives content and direction to his life, he is bound to overrate not only the power of love but also his own ability to love. He will mistake his need to hang on to another person for a particularly great ability to love, and will take a special pride in this illusory capacity. Finally, if C's neurotic trend is to master any situation by his own efforts, to be self-sufficient at any price, he will take an excessive pride in being capable and self-reliant and in never needing anybody.

The maintenance of these beliefs—A's belief in his superior power of reasoning, B's in his loving nature, C's in his competence to handle his affairs quite by himself—becomes as compulsive as the neurotic trends that produced them. But the pride taken in these qualities is sensitive and vulnerable, and for good reasons. Its foundation is none too solid. It is built on too narrow a basis and contains too many illusory elements. It is actually a pride in the qualities that are required in the service of the neurotic trends rather than in qualities actually existing. In actual fact B has very little ability to love, but his belief in this quality is indispensable lest he recognize the falseness of his pursuits. If he harbored any doubt as to his loving nature he would have to recognize that in reality he searches not for someone to love but for someone who will devote his life exclusively to him, without his being able to give much in return. This would mean such a vital threat to his security that he would be bound to react to a criticism on this score with a mixture of panic and hostility, one or the other prevailing. Similarly, A will react with extreme irritation to any doubt cast on his good judgment. C, on the other hand, whose pride lies in not needing anybody, must feel irritated at any suggestion that he cannot succeed without help or advice. The anxiety and hostility generated by such trespasses on the treasured image of self further impair a person's relations to others, and thereby force him to adhere all the more strongly to his protective devices.

Not only the evaluation of self is incisively influenced by the neurotic trends, but also the evaluation of others. The person craving for prestige will judge others exclusively according to the prestige they enjoy: one who enjoys greater prestige he will put above himself, and one with lesser prestige he will look down upon, regardless of the real values involved. The compulsively compliant person is likely to feel indiscriminate adoration of what appears to him as strength, even if this "strength" consists merely in erratic or unscrupulous behavior. The person who must exploit others may take a certain liking to one who lends himself to exploitation, but also despises him; he will think of a compulsively modest person as either stupid or hypocritical. The compulsively dependent person may look enviously at the compulsively self-sufficient person, thinking him free and uninhibited, though actually the latter is merely in the grip of a different neurotic trend.

A last consequence to be discussed here is the inhibitions resulting from the neurotic trends. Inhibitions may be circumscribed, that is, concern a concrete action, sensation, or emotion, taking the form, for example, of impotence or an inhibition toward telephoning. Or they may be diffuse and concern whole areas of life, such as self-assertion, spontaneity, making demands, coming close to people. As a rule specific inhibitions are at the level of awareness. Diffuse inhibitions, though more important, are less tangible.* If they become very strong the person may be generally aware of being inhibited, without, however, recognizing in what specific direction. They may be so subtle and hidden, on the other hand, that the person is not aware of their existence and efficacy. Awareness of inhibitions may be befogged in various ways, of which one of the commonest is rationalization: a person who has inhibitions about speaking to others in social gatherings may be aware of being inhibited on this score, but also he may simply believe that he dislikes parties

* See H. Schultz-Hencke, *Der gehemmte Mensch.*

66

and considers them boring, and find many good reasons for refusing invitations.

The inhibitions produced by neurotic trends are primarily of the diffuse kind. Let us for the sake of clarity compare the person obsessed by a neurotic trend with a rope dancer. The latter, in order to reach the other end of the rope without falling down, must avoid any glance to right or left and must keep his attention fixed on the rope. Here we would not speak of an inhibition to glancing aside, because the rope dancer has a clear recognition of the danger involved and consciously avoids that danger. A person in the clutches of a neurotic trend must equally anxiously avoid any deviation from the prescribed course, but in his case there is an important difference, for with him the process is unconscious: strong inhibitions prevent him from wavering in the course laid down for him.

Thus a person who makes himself dependent on a partner will be inhibited from making independent moves of his own; a person tending toward a constriction of life will be inhibited from having, and still more from asserting, any expansive wishes; a person with a neurotic need to control self and others by reason will be inhibited from feeling any strong emotion; and a person with a compulsive craving for prestige will be inhibited from dancing or speaking in public or from any other activity that might jeopardize his prestige, and in fact his whole learning faculty may be paralyzed because it is intolerable for him to appear awkward during the beginning period. Different as they are, all these inhibitions have an attribute in common: all of them represent a check on any spontaneity of feeling, thought, and action. One can have no more than a studied spontaneity when dancing on a rope. And the panic that seizes a neurotic person if something leads him to trespass his determined boundaries is no less acute than that experienced by the rope dancer who loses his footing.

Thus each neurotic trend generates not only a specific anxiety but also specific types of behavior, a specific image of self and others, a specific pride, a specific kind of vulnerability and specific inhibitions.

So far we have simplified matters by assuming that any one person has only one neurotic trend or a combination of kindred trends. It has been pointed out that a trend toward relegating one's life to a partner is often combined with a general need for affection and with a trend toward constricting one's life within narrow limits; that a craving for power so frequently goes with a craving for prestige that the two may appear as two aspects of the same trend; that an insistence on absolute independence and self-sufficiency is often intertwined with a belief that life can be mastered through reason and foresight. In these instances the coexistence of various trends does not essentially complicate the picture, because while the different trends may collide at times—the need to be admired, for instance, may collide with a need to dominate—their objectives are nevertheless not too far apart. This does not mean that there are no conflicts: each neurotic trend carries within itself the germ of conflicts. But when the trends are kindred the conflicts are manageable

68

by way of repressions, avoidances, and the like, though at great expense to the individual.

The situation changes essentially when a person has developed several neurotic trends that are incompatible in nature. His position then is comparable to that of a servant who is dependent on two masters who give contradictory commands, both expecting blind obedience. If compliance is just as compulsive for him as absolute independence he feels caught in a conflict which does not permit of any permanent solution. He will grope for compromise solutions, but clashes will be inevitable; one pursuit is bound to interfere constantly with its opposite. The same impasse occurs when a compulsive need to dominate others in a dictatorial fashion is combined with a striving to lean on another person, or when a need to exploit others, which precludes the person's productivity, is of equal intensity with a need to be admired as the superior, protective genius. It occurs, in fact, whenever contradictory trends exist together.

The neurotic "symptoms," such as phobias, depressions, alcoholism, ultimately result from these conflicts. The more thoroughly we recognize this fact the less will we be tempted to interpret the symptoms directly. If they are a result of conflicting trends it is as good as useless to try to understand them without having previously gained an understanding of the underlying structure.

It should now be clear that the essence of a "neurosis" is the neurotic character structure, the focal points of which are the neurotic trends. Each of them is the nucleus of a structure within the personality, and each of these substructures is interrelated in many ways with other substructures. It is not only of theoretical interest but of eminent practical importance to realize the nature and complexity of this character structure. Even psychiatrists, not to speak of laymen, tend to underrate the intricacies of the nature of modern man.

The neurotic character structure is more or less rigid, but it is also precarious and vulnerable because of its many weak spots—its pretenses, self-deceptions, and illusions. At innumerable points, the nature of which varies in each individual, its failure to function is noticeable. The person himself senses deeply that something is fundamentally wrong, though he does not know what it is. He may vigorously assert that everything is all right, apart from his headaches or his eating sprees, but he registers deep down that something is wrong.

Not only is he ignorant of the source of trouble, but he has considerable interest in remaining ignorant, because, as emphasized above, his neurotic trends have a definite subjective value for him. In this situation there are two courses he may take: he may, despite the subjective value of his neurotic trends, examine the nature and causes of the deficiencies they produce; or he may deny that anything is wrong or can be changed.

In analysis both courses are followed, one or the other prevailing at different times. The more indispensable the neurotic trends are for a person, and the more questionable their actual value, the more vigorously and rigidly must he defend and justify them. This situation is comparable to the need of a government to defend and justify its activities. The more debatable the government, the less can it tolerate criticism and the more must it assert its rights. These self-justifications constitute what I should like to call secondary defenses. Their purpose is not only to defend one or another questionable factor but to safeguard the maintenance of the whole neurotic structure. They are like a minefield laid out around the neurosis for its protection. Different though they appear in detail, their common denominator is a persuasion that in essence everything is right, good, or unalterable.

It is in accord with the comprehensive function of the secondary defenses that the attitudes they entail tend to be generalized in order not to leave open any loophole. Thus, for example, a person who has surrounded himself with an armor of self-righteousness will not only defend his power drive as right, rational, and warranted, but will be unable to admit that anything he does, trivial though it may be, is wrong or questionable. The secondary defenses may be so hidden that they can be detected only during analytical work, or they may constitute a prominent feature of the observable picture of the personality; they are easily recognized, for instance, in the person who must always be right. They must not necessarily appear as a character trait but may take the form of moral or scientific convictions; thus an overemphasis on constitutional factors often represents a person's conviction that he is as he is "by nature," and that hence everything is unalterable. Also the intensity and rigidity of these defenses vary considerably. In Clare, for instance, whose analysis we follow throughout the book, they played hardly any role. In others they may be so strong as to render any attempt at analysis impossible. The more a person is intent upon maintaining the *status quo* the more impenetrable are his defenses. But while there are variations in transparency, intensity, and manifestations, the secondary defenses, in contrast to the manifold shades and variations of the neurotic character structure itself, show a monotonous repetition of the themes "good," "right," "unalterable," in one or another combination.

I should like now to return to my initial assertion that neurotic trends are in the center of psychic disturbances. This statement does not mean, of course, that the neurotic trends are what the individual feels most keenly as disturbances: as mentioned before, he is usually unaware that they are the driving forces in his life. Nor does it mean that the neurotic trends are the ultimate source of all psychic troubles: the trends themselves are a product of previous disturbances, conflicts that have occurred in human relationships. My contention is rather that the focal point in the whole neurotic structure is what I have called the neurotic trends. They provide a way out of the initial calamities, offering a promise that life can be coped with despite disturbed relationships to self and others. But also they produce a great variety of new disturbances: illusions about the world and about the self, vulnerabilities, inhibitions, conflicts. They are at the same time a solution of initial difficulties and a source of further ones.

CHAPTER THREE

Stages of Psychoanalytic Understanding

A knowledge of the neurotic trends and their implications gives a rough conception of what has to be worked through in analysis. It is also desirable, however, to know something about the sequence in which the work must be done. Are problems tackled in a helter-skelter fashion? Does one obtain a piecemeal insight here and there until at last the pieces of the jigsaw puzzle are put together into an understandable picture? Or are there principles that may serve as a guide in the maze of material offering itself?

Freud's answer to this question seems easy enough. Freud declared that a person will first present in the analysis the same front that he presents to the world in general, and that then his repressed strivings will gradually appear, in succession from the less repressed to the more repressed. If we were to take a bird's-eye view of the

73

analytical procedure this answer would still hold true. And even as a guide for action the general principle involved would be good enough if the findings to be made lay around a single vertical line along which we would have to wind our way into the depths. But if we should assume that this is the case, if we should assume that if we only continue to analyze whatever material shows up we shall penetrate step by step into *the* repressed area, we may easily find ourselves in a state of confusion—which indeed happens not infrequently.

The theory of neuroses developed in the previous chapter gives us more specific leads. It holds that there are several focal points in the neurotic personality given by the neurotic trends and the structure built around each of them. The inference to be drawn for the therapeutic procedure is, briefly, that we must discover each trend and each time descend into the depths. More concretely, the implications of each neurotic trend are repressed in various degrees. Those that are less deeply repressed are the first to become accessible; those that are more deeply repressed will emerge later. The extensive example of self-analysis presented in Chapter Eight will illustrate this point.

The same principle applies to the order in which the neurotic trends themselves can be tackled. One patient will start by presenting the implications of his need for absolute independence and superiority, and only much later can one discover and tackle indications of his compliance or of his need for affection. The next patient will start with an open display of his need to be loved and approved of, and his tendencies to control others, if he has any, could not possibly be approached at the beginning; but a third one will from the beginning display a highly developed power drive. The fact that a trend appears at the beginning indicates nothing about its comparative importance or unimportance: the neurotic trend that appears first is not necessarily the strongest one in the sense of having the greatest influence on the personality. We could rather say that that trend is the first to crystallize which jibes best with the person's conscious or semiconscious image of himself. If secondary defenses—the means of self-justification—are highly developed they may entirely dominate the picture at the beginning. In that case the neurotic trends become visible and accessible only later on.

I should like to illustrate the stages of understanding with the example of the patient Clare whose childhood history was briefly outlined in the previous chapter. When the analysis is reported for this purpose it must, of course, be grossly simplified and schematized. I must leave out not only many details and ramifications but also all the difficulties encountered during the analytical work. Moreover, the various phases appear, in summary, more clear cut than they actually were: factors that appear in the report as belonging to the first phase, for instance, actually emerged then only dimly and became clearer throughout the analysis. I believe, however, that these inaccuracies do not essentially detract from the validity of the principles presented.

Clare came for analytic treatment at the age of thirty, for various reasons. She was easily overcome by a paralyzing fatigue that interfered with her work and her social life. Also, she complained about having remarkably little self-confidence. She was the editor of a magazine, and though her professional career and her present position were satisfactory her ambition to write plays and stories was checked by insurmountable inhibitions. She could do her routine work but was unable to do productive work, though she was inclined to account for this latter inability by pointing out her probable lack of talent. She had been married at the age of twenty-three, but the husband had died after three years. After the marriage she had had a relationship with another man which continued during the analysis. According to her initial presentation both relationships were satisfactory sexually as well as otherwise.

The analysis stretched over a period of four and a half years. She was analyzed for one year and a half. This time was followed by an interruption of two years, in which she did a good deal of self-analysis, afterward returning to analysis for another year at irregular intervals.

Clare's analysis could be roughly divided into three phases: the discovery of her compulsive modesty; the discovery of her compulsive dependence on a partner; and finally, the discovery of her compulsive need to force others to recognize her superiority. None of these trends was apparent to herself or to others.

In the first period the data that suggested compulsive elements were as follows. She tended to minimize her own value and capacities: not only was she insecure about her assets but she tenaciously denied their existence, insisting that she was not intelligent, attractive, or gifted and tending to discard evidence to the contrary. Also, she tended to regard others as superior to herself. If there was a dissension of opinion she automatically believed that the others were right. She recalled that when her husband had started an affair with another woman she did nothing to remonstrate against it, though the experience was extremely painful to her; she managed to consider him justified in preferring the other on the grounds that the latter was more attractive and more loving. Moreover, it was almost impossible for her to spend money on herself: when she traveled with others she could enjoy living in expensive places, even though she contributed her share in the expenses, but as soon as she was on her own she could not bring herself to spend money on such things as trips, dresses, plays, books. Finally, though she was in an executive position, it was impossible for her to give orders: she would do so in an apologetic way if orders were unavoidable.

The conclusion reached from such data was that she had developed a compulsive modesty, that she felt compelled to constrict her life within narrow boundaries and to take always a second or third place. When this trend was once recognized, and its origin in childhood discussed, we began to search systematically for its manifestations and its consequences. What role did this trend actually play in her life?

She could not assert herself in any way. In discussions

77

she was easily swayed by the opinions of others. Despite a good faculty for judging people she was incapable of taking any critical stand toward anyone or anything, except in editing, when a critical stand was expected of her. She had encountered serious difficulties, for instance, by failing to realize that a fellow worker was trying to undermine her position; when this situation was fully apparent to others she still regarded the other as her friend. Her compulsion to take second place appeared clearly in games: in tennis, for instance, she was usually too inhibited to play well, but occasionally she was able to play a good game and then, as soon as she became aware that she might win, she would begin to play badly. The wishes of others were more important than her own: she would be contented to take her holidays during the time that was least wanted by others, and she would do more work than she needed to if the others were dissatisfied with the amount of work to be done.

Most important was a general suppression of her feelings and wishes. Her inhibitions concerning expansive plans she regarded as particularly "realistic"—evidence that she never wanted things that were beyond reach. Actually she was as little "realistic" as someone with excessive expectations of life; she merely kept her wishes beneath the level of the attainable. She was unrealistic in living in every way beneath her means—socially, economically, professionally, spiritually. It was attainable for her, as her later life showed, to be liked by many people, to look attractive, to write something that was valuable and original.

78

The most general consequences of this trend were a progressive lowering of self-confidence and a diffuse discontentment with life. Of the latter she had not been in the least aware, and could not be aware as long as everything was "good enough" for her and she was not clearly conscious of having wishes or of their not being fulfilled. The only way this general discontentment with life had shown itself was in trivial matters and in sudden spells of crying which had occurred from time to time and which had been quite beyond her understanding.

For quite a while she recognized only fragmentarily the truth of these findings; in important matters she made the silent reservation that I either overrated her or felt it to be good therapy to encourage her. Finally, however, she recognized in a rather dramatic fashion that real, intense anxiety lurked behind this façade of modesty. It was at a time when she was about to suggest an improvement in the magazine. She knew that her plan was good, that it would not meet with too much opposition, that everyone would be appreciative in the end. Before suggesting it, however, she had an intense panic which could not be rationalized in any way. At the beginning of the discussion she still felt panicky and had to leave the room because of a sudden diarrhea. But as the discussion turned increasingly in her favor the panic subsided. The plan was finally accepted and she received considerable recognition. She went home with a feeling of elation and was still in good spirits when she came to the next analytical hour.

I dropped a casual remark to the effect that this was

quite a triumph for her, which she rejected with a slight annoyance. Naturally she had enjoyed the recognition but her prevailing feeling was one of having escaped from a great danger. It was only after more than two years had elapsed that she could tackle the other elements involved in this experience, which were along the lines of ambition, dread of failure, triumph. At that time her feelings, as expressed in her associations, were all concentrated on the problem of modesty. She felt that she had been presumptuous to propound a new plan. Who was she to know better! But gradually she realized that this attitude was based on the fact that for her the suggesting of a different course of action meant a venturing out of the narrow artificial precincts that she had anxiously preserved. Only when she recognized the truth of this observation did she become fully convinced that her modesty was a façade to be maintained for the sake of safety. The result of this first phase of work was a beginning of faith in herself and a beginning of courage to feel and assert her wishes and opinions.

The second period was dedicated prevailingly to work on her dependency on a "partner." The majority of the problems involved she worked through by herself, as will be reported later on in greater detail. This dependency, despite its overwhelming strength, was still more deeply repressed than the previous trend. It had never occurred to her that anything was wrong in her relationships with men. On the contrary, she had believed them to be particularly good. The analysis gradually changed this picture.

There were three main factors that suggested compulsive dependence. The first was that she felt completely lost, like a small child in a strange wood, when a relationship ended or when she was temporarily separated from a person who was important to her. The first experience of this kind occurred after she left home at the age of twenty. She then felt like a feather blown around in the universe, and she wrote desperate letters to her mother, declaring that she could not live without her. This homesickness stopped when she developed a kind of crush on an older man, a successful writer who was interested in her work and furthered her in a patronizing way. Of course, this first experience of feeling lost when alone could be understood on the basis of her youth and the sheltered life she had lived. But later reactions were intrinsically the same, and formed a strange contrast to the rather successful professional career that she was achieving despite the difficulties mentioned before.

The second striking fact was that in any of these relationships the whole world around her became submerged and only the beloved had any importance. Thoughts and feelings centered around a call or a letter or a visit from him; hours that she spent without him were empty, filled only with waiting for him, with a pondering about his attitude to her, and above all with feeling utterly miserable about incidents which she felt as utter neglect or humiliating rejection. At these times other human relationships, her work, and other interests lost almost every value for her.

The third factor was a fantasy of a great and master-ful man whose willing slave she was and who in turn gave her everything she wanted, from an abundance of material things to an abundance of mental stimulation, and made her a famous writer.

As the implications of these factors were gradually recognized the compulsive need to lean on a "partner" appeared and was worked through in its characteristics and its consequences. Its main feature was an entirely repressed parasitic attitude, an unconscious wish to feed on the partner, to expect him to supply the content of her life, to take responsibility for her, to solve all her difficulties and to make her a great person without her having to make efforts of her own. This trend had alien-ated her not only from other people but also from the partner himself, because the unavoidable disappoint-ments she felt when her secret expectations of him re-mained unfulfilled gave rise to a deep inner irritation; most of this irritation was repressed for fear of losing the partner, but some of it emerged in occasional explosions. Another consequence was that she could not enjoy any-thing except when she shared it with the partner. The most general consequence of this trend was that her re-lationships served only to make her more insecure and more passive and to breed self-contempt.

The interrelations of this trend with the previous one were twofold. On the one hand, her compulsive mod-esty was one of the reasons that accounted for her need for a partner. Since she could not take care of her own wishes she had to have someone else who took care of them. Since she could not defend herself she needed someone else to defend her. Since she could not see her own values she needed someone else to affirm her worth. On the other hand, there was a sharp conflict between the compulsive modesty and the excessive expectations of the partner. Because of this unconscious conflict she had to distort the situation every time she was disappointed over unfulfilled expectations. In such situations she felt herself the victim of intolerably harsh and abusive treatment, and therefore felt miserable and hostile. Most of the hostility had to be repressed because of fear of desertion, but its existence undermined the relationship and turned her expectations into vindictive demands. The resulting upsets proved to have a great bearing on her fatigue and her inhibition toward productive work.

The result of this period of analytical work was that she overcame her parasitic helplessness and became capable of greater activity of her own. The fatigue was no longer continual but appeared only occasionally. She became capable of writing, though she still had to face strong resistances. Her relationships with people became more friendly, though they were still far from being spontaneous; she impressed others as being haughty while she herself still felt quite timid. An expression of the general change in her was contained in a dream in which she drove with her friend in a strange country and it occurred to her that she, too, might apply for a driver's license. Actually, she had a license and could drive as well as the friend. The dream symbolized a dawning insight that she had rights of her own and need not feel like a helpless appendage.

The third and last period of analytical work dealt with repressed ambitious strivings. There had been a period in her life when she had been obsessed by frantic ambition. This had lasted from her later years in grammar school up to her second year in college, and had then seemed to disappear. One could conclude only by inference that it still operated underground. This was suggested by the fact that she was elated and overjoyed at any recognition, by her dread of failure, and by the anxiety involved in any attempt at independent work.

This trend was more complicated in its structure than the two others. In contrast to the others, it constituted an attempt to master life actively, to take up a fight against adverse forces. This fact was one element in its continued existence: she felt herself that there had been a positive force in her ambition and wished repeatedly to be able to retrieve it. A second element feeding the ambition was the necessity to re-establish her lost self-esteem. The third element was vindictiveness: success meant a triumph over all those who had humiliated her, while failure meant disgraceful defeat. To understand the characteristics of this ambition we must go back in her history and discover the successive changes it underwent.

The fighting spirit involved in this trend appeared

quite early in life. Indeed, it preceded the development of the other two trends. At this period of the analysis early memories occurred to her of opposition, rebellion, belligerent demands, all sorts of mischief. As we know, she lost this fight for her place in the sun because the odds against her were too great. Then, after a series of unhappy experiences, this spirit re-emerged when she was about eleven, in the form of a fierce ambition at school. Now, however, it was loaded with repressed hostility: it had absorbed the piled-up vindictiveness for the unfair deal she had received and for her downtrodden dignity. It had now acquired two of the elements mentioned above: through being on top she would re-establish her sunken self-confidence, and by defeating the others she would avenge her injuries. This grammar-school ambition, with all its compulsive and destructive elements, was nevertheless realistic in comparison with later developments, for it entailed efforts to surpass others through greater actual achievements. During high school she was still successful in being unquestionably the first. But in college, where she met greater competition, she rather suddenly dropped her ambition altogether, instead of making the greater efforts that the situation would have required if she still wanted to be first. There were three main reasons why she could not muster the courage to make these greater efforts. One was that because of her compulsive modesty she had to fight against constant doubts as to her intelligence. Another was the actual impairment in the free use of her intelligence through the repression of her

85

The consequences of this trend were worked through by recognizing the influence they had on her attitude toward life in general, toward work, toward others, and toward herself. The outstanding result of this examination was a diminution of her inhibitions toward work.

We then tackled the interrelations of this trend with the two others. There were, on the one hand, irreconcilable conflicts and, on the other hand, mutual reinforcements, evidence of how inextricably she was caught in her neurotic structure. Conflicts existed between the compulsion to assume a humble place and to triumph over others, between ambition to excel and parasitic dependency, the two drives necessarily clashing and either arousing anxiety or paralyzing each other. This paralyzing effect proved to be one of the deepest sources of the fatigue as well as of the inhibitions toward work. No less important, however, were the ways in which the trends reinforced one another. To be modest and to put herself into a humble place became all the more necessary as it served also as a cloak for the need for triumph. The partner, as already mentioned, became an all the more vital necessity as he had also to satisfy in a devious way the need for triumph. Moreover, the feelings of humiliation generated by the need to live beneath her emotional and mental capacities and by her dependency on the partner kept evoking new feelings of vindictiveness, and thus perpetuated and reinforced the need for triumph.

The analytical work consisted in disrupting step by step the vicious circles operating. The fact that her compulsive modesty had already given way to some measure of self-assertion was of great help because this progress automatically lessened also the need for triumph. Similarly, the partial solution of the dependency problem, having made her stronger and having removed many feelings of humiliation, made the need for triumph less stringent. Thus when she finally approached the issue of vindictiveness, which was deeply shocking to her, she could tackle with increased inner strength an already diminished problem. To have tackled it at the beginning would not have been feasible. In the first place we would not have understood it, and in the second place she could not have stood it.

The result of this last period was a general liberation of energies. Clare retrieved her lost ambition on a much sounder basis. It was now less compulsive and less destructive; its emphasis shifted from an interest in success to an interest in the subject matter. Her relationships with people, already improved after the second period, now lost the tenseness created by the former mixture of a false humility and a defensive haughtiness.

With all due reservation for the oversimplifications mentioned above, I believe, from experience, that this report illustrates the typical course of an analysis, or, to put it more cautiously, the ideal course of an analysis. The fact that there were three main divisions in Clare's analysis is only incidental; there may just as well be two or five. It is characteristic, however, that in each division the analysis passed through three steps: recognition

of a neurotic trend; discovery of its causes, manifestations, and consequences; and discovery of its interrelations with other parts of the personality, especially with
other neurotic trends. These steps must be taken for
each neurotic trend involved. Each time a step is worked
through part of the structure becomes clearer until finally the whole emerges transparent. The steps are not
always taken in the order named; more precisely, some
understanding of a trend's manifestations is necessary
before the trend itself can be recognized as such. This is
well illustrated in Clare's self-analysis, to be reported in
Chapter Eight. Clare recognized many important implications of her morbid dependency before she recognized the fact of being dependent and the powerful urge
driving her into a dependent relationship.

Each of the steps has a particular therapeutic value.
The first step, the recognition of a neurotic trend, means
the recognition of a driving force in the disturbance of
the personality, and this knowledge in itself has a certain
value for therapy. Formerly the person felt powerless, at
the mercy of intangible forces. The recognition of even
one of these forces not only means a general gain in insight but also dispels some of the bewildered helplessness. Knowledge of the concrete reason for a disturbance
provides a realization that there is a chance to do something about it. This change may be illustrated with a
simple example. A farmer wants to grow fruit trees, but
his trees do not thrive, though he puts great efforts into
their care and tries all the remedies he knows. After
some time he becomes discouraged. But finally he dis-

89

covers that the trees have a special disease or need a special ingredient in the soil, and there is an immediate change in his outlook on the matter and his mood regarding it, though nothing has changed as yet in the trees themselves. The only difference in the external situation is that there is now a possibility of goal-directed action.

Sometimes the mere uncovering of a neurotic trend is sufficient to cure a neurotic upset. A capable executive, for instance, was deeply disturbed because the attitude of his employees, which had always been one of devotion, changed for reasons outside his control. Instead of settling differences in an amicable way, they started to make belligerent and unreasonable demands. Although he was a highly resourceful person in most matters he felt utterly incapable of coping with this new situation, and reached such a measure of resentment and despair that he considered withdrawing from the business. In this instance the mere uncovering of his deep need for the devotion of people dependent on him sufficed to remedy the situation.

Usually, however, the mere recognition of a neurotic trend does not engender any radical change. In the first place, the willingness to change which is elicited by the discovery of such a trend is equivocal and hence lacks forcefulness, and, in the second place, a willingness to change, even if it amounts to an unambiguous wish, is not yet an ability to change. This ability develops only later.

The reason why the initial willingness to overcome a

neurotic trend does not usually constitute a reliable force, despite the enthusiasm that often goes with it, is that the trend has also a subjective value which the person does not want to relinquish. When the prospect arises of overcoming a particular compulsive need, those forces are mobilized which want to maintain it. In other words, soon after the first liberating effect of the discovery the person is confronted with a conflict: he wants to change and he does not want to change. This conflict usually remains unconscious because he does not like to admit that he wants to adhere to something which is against reason and self-interest.

If for any reason the determination not to change prevails, the liberating effect of the discovery will be only a fleeting relief followed by a deeper discouragement. To return to the analogy of the farmer, his change in spirit will not last long if he knows or believes that the required remedy is not available to him.

Fortunately these negative reactions are not too frequent. More often the willingness and the unwillingness to change tend to compromise. The patient then sticks to his resolution to change, but wants to get away with as little as possible. He may hope that it will be enough if he uncovers the origin of the trend in childhood, or if he merely makes resolutions to change, or he may fall back on the delusion that a mere recognition of the trend will change everything overnight.

In the second step, however, as he works through the implications of the trend, he realizes more and more deeply its unfortunate consequences, the degree to which it cramps his life in all respects. Suppose, for example, that he has a neurotic need for absolute independence. After recognizing the trend and learning something of its origins he would have to spend quite a while understanding why only this way is open for reassurance, and how it manifests itself in his daily living. He would have to see in detail how this need expresses itself in his attitude toward physical surroundings, how it takes the form, perhaps, of an aversion to obstructed views, or an anxiety that arises when he sits in the middle of a row. He would have to know how it influences his attitude toward dress, as evidenced by such signs as sensitivity toward girdles, shoes, neckties, or anything that may be felt as a constriction. He would have to recognize the influence of the trend on work, shown perhaps in a rebellion against routine, obligations, expectations, suggestions, a rebellion against time and against superiors. He would have to understand its influence on love life, observing such factors as an incapacity to accept any ties or a tendency to feel that any interest in another person means enslavement. Thus an estimate would gradually crystallize as to the various factors which in greater or less degree serve to touch off the feeling of coercion and to force him to be on his guard. The mere knowledge that he has a great wish for independence is not nearly enough. It is only when he recognizes its all-inclusive compelling force and its negativistic character that he can muster a serious incentive to change.

Thus the therapeutic value of the second step is, first, that it strengthens a person's willingness to conquer the

disturbing drive. He begins to appreciate the full necessity for change, and his rather equivocal willingness to
overcome the disturbance turns into an unambiguous
determination to grapple with it seriously.

This determination certainly constitutes a powerful
and valuable force, indispensable for effecting any
change. But even the most vigorous determination is
of little avail without the ability to carry it through.
And this ability is gradually increased as one manifestation after another is clearly seen. While a person is
working at the implications of the neurotic trend his
illusions, fears, vulnerabilities, and inhibitions are gradually loosened from their entrenchments. As a result he
becomes less insecure, less isolated, less hostile, and the
resultant improvement in his relationships with others,
and with himself, in turn makes the neurotic trend less
necessary and increases his capacity to deal with it.

This part of the work has the added value of kindling
an incentive to discover those factors that impede a more
profound change. The forces thus far mobilized have
helped to dissolve the power of the particular trend and
thereby to bring about certain improvements. But the
trend itself and many of its implications are almost sure
to be closely bound up with other, possibly contradictory, drives. Therefore the person cannot fully overcome
his difficulties by working only at the substructure developed around a particular trend. Clare, for instance,
lost some of her compulsive modesty through the analysis of that trend, but certain of its implications were
out of reach at that time because they were intertwined

with the morbid dependency and could be tackled only in conjunction with that further problem.

This third step, the recognition and understanding of the interrelations of different neurotic trends, leads to a grasp on the deepest conflicts. It means an understanding of the attempts at solutions and of how these attempts have meant only a deeper and deeper entanglement. Before this part of the work is reached the person may have gained a deep insight into the component parts of a conflict, but still have adhered secretly to a belief that they could be reconciled. He may have realized deeply, for instance, the nature of his drive to be despotic and also the nature of his need to be applauded for superior wisdom. But he has tried to reconcile these trends by simply admitting occasionally the despotic drive without having the least intention to change it. He has expected secretly that the admission of the despotic trend would allow him to continue it and at the same time win him recognition for the amount of insight shown. Another person who strove for superhuman serenity, but also was driven by vindictive impulses, has imagined that he could be serene for the larger part of the year but spare out a sort of leave of absence when he could indulge in his vindictiveness. It is obvious that no fundamental change can take place as long as such solutions are secretly adhered to. As the third step is worked through it becomes possible to understand the makeshift nature of these solutions.

The therapeutic value of this step lies also in the fact that it makes it possible to disentangle the vicious circles

94

operating among the various neurotic trends, the ways in which they reinforce one another as well as the ways in which they conflict with one another. Thus it means an understanding at last of the so-called symptoms, that is, the gross pathological manifestations, such as attacks of anxiety, phobias, depressions, /gross compulsions.|

One often hears statements to the effect that what is really important in psychotherapy is to see the conflicts. Such statements are of the same value as a contention that what is really important is the neurotic vulnerability or rigidity or striving for superiority. What is important is to see the whole structure, not more and not less. Existing conflicts may sometimes be recognized quite early in the analysis. Such recognition, however, is of no avail until the components of the conflicts are thoroughly understood and diminished in their intensity. Only after this work has been accomplished do the conflicts themselves become accessible.

Let us finish this discussion by asking for the practical value of the information presented in this and the preceding chapter. Does it give definite and detailed directions as to the road to be taken in analysis? The answer is that no amount of knowledge can fulfill such expectations. One reason for this is that the differences among people are too great to allow the pursuit of any prescribed path. Even if we should assume that there is but a limited number of discernible neurotic trends existing in our civilization, say fifteen, the possible combinations of such trends would be practically infinite. Another reason is that in analysis we see not one trend neatly separated from another, but the sum total of entanglements; a flexible ingenuity is therefore necessary in order to isolate the components of the picture. A third complication is that often the consequences of the various trends are not apparent as such but are themselves repressed, thus making recognition of the trend considerably difficult. And, finally, analysis represents a human relationship as well as a common research. It would be a one-sided comparison to think of an analysis as an exploratory trip in which two colleagues or friends are engaged, both as much interested in observing and understanding as in integrating the observations and drawing the inferences. In analysis the patient's peculiarities and disturbances—not to speak of the analyst's—are vitally important. His need for affection, his pride, his vulnerability, are just as present and as effective in this as in other situations, and in addition the analysis itself inevitably elicits anxieties and hostilities and defenses against insights that threaten his safety system or the pride he has developed. While all these reactions are helpful, provided one understands them, they nevertheless render the process more complex and less susceptible of generalization.

The assertion that to a large extent each analysis must produce its own sequence for tackling problems may be intimidating to apprehensive souls, particularly to those who need a guarantee that they are always doing the right thing. They should keep in mind, however, for their own reassurance, that this sequence is not artificially created by the analyst's clever manipulation but occurs spontaneously because it lies in the nature of the problems that one becomes accessible after another one is solved. In other words, when anyone analyzes himself he will usually take the steps described above by merely following the material that presents itself. It will sometimes happen, of course, that he touches upon questions that at the time being are not answerable. At such points an experienced analyst will probably be able to see that the particular subject is beyond the reach of the patient's understanding and is therefore better left alone. Let us assume, for instance, that a patient who is still deeply immersed in convictions of his absolute superiority over others brings up material suggesting that he has a fear of not being acceptable to others. The analyst will know that it would be premature to tackle as yet the patient's fear of rejection, because the latter would regard it as inconceivable that such a superior being as he believes himself to be could possibly have such a fear. Many other times the analyst will recognize only in retrospect that, and why, a problem was not accessible at a certain point. In other words, he, too, can proceed only by trial and error.

In self-analysis it may even be that there is less temptation to tackle a factor prematurely, because the person will intuitively shirk a problem that he is not yet able to face. But if he does notice, after grappling with a problem for some time, that he is not getting any nearer to a solution, he should remember that he may not yet be ready to work at it and that perhaps he had better leave

97

it alone for the time being. And he need not be discouraged at this turn of events, for very often even a premature attack provides a significant lead for further work. It need hardly be emphasized, however, that there may be other reasons why a solution that presents itself is not accepted, and he should not resort too quickly to the assumption that it is merely premature.

And information of the kind I have presented is helpful not only in forestalling unnecessary discouragement but also in more positive ways, for it helps one to integrate and understand peculiarities which otherwise would remain disconnected observations. A person may realize, for example, that he finds difficulties in asking for anything, from inquiring the right way on a motor trip to consulting a doctor for an illness, that he conceals his going to analysis as if it were a disgrace, a despicable easy road, because he feels he should be able to deal with his problems all by himself, that he becomes irritated if anyone shows him sympathy or offers advice and feels humiliated if he must accept help; and if he has some knowledge of neurotic trends the possibility will occur to him that all these reactions emanate from an underlying trend toward compulsive self-sufficiency. Naturally, there is no guarantee that the surmise is right. The assumption that he is generally weary of people might explain some of his reactions, though it would not account for the feeling of hurt pride that arises on some occasions. Any surmise must be made tentatively and kept in abeyance until he has plenty of evidence for its validity. Even then he must ascertain over and over again whether the assumption really covers the ground or is only partially valid. Naturally, he can never expect that one trend will explain everything: he must remember that there will be countercurrents. All he can reasonably expect is that the trend surmised represents one of the compelling forces in his life and therefore must reveal itself in a consistent pattern of reactions.

His knowledge will be of positive help also after he has recognized a neurotic trend. An understanding of the therapeutic importance of discovering the various manifestations and consequences of a trend will help him to focus attention deliberately on these instead of getting lost in a frantic search for the reasons of its power, most of which can be understood only later on. Such an understanding will be particularly valuable in directing his thoughts toward a gradual recognition of the price paid for the pursuit of the trend.

In regard to the conflicts the practical value of psychological knowledge lies in the fact that it prevents the individual from merely shuttling to and fro between disparate attitudes. Clare, for instance, at the time when she analyzed herself, lost considerable time shuttling between a tendency to put all blame on others and a tendency to put all blame on herself. Thus she became confused because she wanted to solve the question which of these contradictory tendencies she really had, or at least which was prevailing. Actually, both were present and emerged from contradictory neurotic trends. The tendency to find fault with herself and to recoil from accusing others was one of the results of her compulsive

99

modesty. The tendency to put the blame on others resulted from her need to feel superior, which made it intolerable for her to recognize any shortcomings of her own. If at this time she had thought of the possibility of conflicting trends, arising from conflicting sources, she might have grasped the process a good deal earlier.

Thus far we have briefly surveyed the structure of neuroses and have discussed the general way in which the unconscious forces must be tackled in order to obtain gradually a lucid picture of the whole structure. We have as yet not touched upon specific means of unearthing them. In the following two chapters we shall discuss the work that patient and analyst must do in order to arrive eventually at an understanding of the patient's personality.

CHAPTER FOUR

The Patient's Share
in the Psychoanalytic Process

Self-analysis is an attempt to be patient and analyst at the same time, and therefore it is desirable to discuss the tasks of each of these participants in the analytic process. It should be borne in mind, however, that this process is not only the sum of the work done by the analyst and the work done by the patient, but is also a human relationship. The fact that there are two persons involved has considerable influence on the work done by each.

There are three main tasks that confront the patient. Of these the first is to express himself as completely and frankly as possible. The second is to become aware of his unconscious driving forces and their influence on his life. And the third is to develop the capacity to change those attitudes that are disturbing his relations with himself and the world around him.

Complete self-expression is achieved by means of free association. It was Freud's ingenious discovery that free association, hitherto used only for psychological experiments, could be utilized in therapy. To associate freely means an endeavor on the part of the patient to express without reserve, and in the sequence in which it emerges, everything that comes into his mind, regardless of whether it is or appears trivial, off the point, incoherent, irrational, indiscreet, tactless, embarrassing, humiliating. It may not be unnecessary to add that "everything" is meant literally. It includes not only fleeting and diffuse thoughts but also specific ideas and memories—incidents that have occurred since the last interview, memories of experiences at any period of life, thoughts about self and others, reactions to the analyst or the analytical situation, beliefs in regard to religion, morals, politics, art, wishes and plans for the future, fantasies past and present, and, of course, dreams. It is particularly important that the patient express every feeling that emerges, such as fondness, hope, triumph, discouragement, relief, suspicion, anger, as well as every diffuse or specific thought. Of course the patient will have objections to voicing certain things, for one reason or another, but he should express these objections instead of using them to withhold the particular thought or feeling.

Free association differs from our customary way of thinking or talking not only in its frankness and unreservedness, but also in its apparent lack of direction. In discussing a problem, talking about our plans for the week end, explaining the value of merchandise to a customer, we are accustomed to stick fairly closely to the point. From the diverse currents that pass through our minds we tend to select those elements for expression which are pertinent to the situation. Even when talking with our closest friends we select what to express and what to omit, even though we are not aware of it. In free association, however, there is an effort to express everything that passes through the mind, regardless of where it may lead.

Like many other human endeavors, free association can be used for constructive or for obstructive purposes. If the patient has an unambiguous determination to reveal himself to the analyst his associations will be meaningful and suggestive. If he has stringent interests not to face certain unconscious factors his associations will be unproductive. These interests may be so prevailing that the good sense of free association is turned into nonsense. What results then is a flight of meaningless ideas having merely a mock resemblance to their true purpose. Thus the value of free association depends entirely on the spirit in which it is done. If the spirit is one of utmost frankness and sincerity, of determination to face one's own problems, and of willingness to open oneself to another human being, then the process can serve the purpose for which it is intended.

In general terms this purpose is to enable both analyst and patient to understand how the latter's mind works and thereby to understand eventually the structure of his personality. There are also specific issues, however, which can be cleared up by free associations—the meaning of an attack of anxiety, of a sudden fatigue, of a fantasy or a dream, why the patient's mind goes blank at a certain point, why he has a sudden wave of resentment toward the analyst, why he was nauseated in the restaurant last night, was impotent with his wife, or was tongue-tied in a discussion. The patient will then try to see what occurs to him when he thinks about the specific issue.

To illustrate, a woman patient had a dream in which one element was a distress about something precious being stolen. I asked her what occurred to her in connection with this particular fragment of the dream. The first association that appeared was a memory of a maid who had stolen household goods over a period of two years; the patient had dimly suspected the maid, and she remembered the deep feeling of uneasiness she had had before the final discovery. The second association was a memory of childhood fears of gypsies stealing children. The next was a mystery story in which jewels had been stolen from the crown of a saint. Then she remembered a remark she had overheard, to the effect that analysts are racketeers. Finally it occurred to her that something in the dream reminded her of the analyst's office.

The associations indicated beyond doubt that the dream was related to the analytical situation. The remark about analysts being racketeers suggested a concern about the fees, but this tack proved to be misleading; she had always regarded the fees as reasonable and worth while. Was the dream a response to the preceding

104

analytical hour? She did not believe that it could be, because she had left the office with a pronounced feeling of relief and gratitude. The substance of the previous analytical session was that she had recognized her periods of listlessness and inertia as a kind of subversive depression; that these periods had not appeared to her or others in this light because she had had no feelings of despondency; that actually she suffered more and was more vulnerable than she admitted to herself; that she had often repressed hurt feelings because she felt compelled to play the role of an ideally strong character who could cope with everything. Her relief had been similar to that of a person who at great expense to himself has lived above his means all his life and now understands for the first time that such a bluff is not necessary. This relief, however, had not lasted. At any rate, it now struck her suddenly that after that session she had been quite irritable, that she had had a slight stomach upset and had been unable to fall asleep.

I shall not go over the associations in detail. The most important clue proved to be the association of the mystery story: I had stolen a jewel out of her crown. The striving to give to herself and others the impression of outstanding strength had been a burden, to be sure, but it had also served several important functions: it gave her a feeling of pride, which she badly needed as long as her real self-confidence was shaken; and it was her most powerful defense against recognizing her existing vulnerability and the irrational trends accounting for it. Thus the role she was playing was actually precious to her, and our uncovering the fact that it was merely a role constituted a threat to which she had reacted with indignation.

Free association would be entirely unfit as a method for making an astronomical calculation or for gaining clarity as to the meaning of a political situation. These tasks require sharp and concise reasoning. But free association constitutes a thoroughly appropriate method— according to our present knowledge, the only method —for understanding the existence, importance, and meaning of unconscious feelings and strivings.

One more word about the value of free association for self-recognition: it does not work magic. It would be wrong to expect that as soon as rational control is released all that we are afraid of or despise in ourselves will be revealed. We may be fairly sure that no more will appear this way than we are able to stand. Only derivatives of the repressed feelings or drives will emerge, and as in dreams they will emerge in distorted form or in symbolic expressions. Thus in the chain of associations mentioned above the saint was an expression of the patient's unconscious aspirations. Of course, unexpected factors will sometimes appear in a dramatic fashion, but this will happen only after considerable previous work on the same subject has brought them close to the surface. Repressed feelings may appear in the form of a seemingly remote memory, as in the chain of associations already described. There the patient's anger at me for having injured her inflated notions about herself did not appear as such; only indirectly she told me that I was like a low criminal who violated holy tabus and robbed values precious to others.

Free associations do not work miracles, but if carried out in the right spirit they do show the way the mind operates, as X-rays show the otherwise invisible movements of lungs or intestines. And they do this in a more or less cryptic language.

To associate freely is difficult for everyone. Not only does it contrast with our habits of communication and with conventional etiquette, but it entails further difficulties which differ with each patient. These may be classified under various headings though they are inevitably overlapping.

In the first place, there are patients in whom the whole process of association arouses fears or inhibitions, because if they should permit free passage to every feeling and thought they would trespass on territory that is tabu. The particular fears that will be touched off depend ultimately on the existing neurotic trends. A few examples may illustrate.

An apprehensive person, overwhelmed since his early years by the threat of the unpredictable dangers of life, is unconsciously set upon avoiding risks. He clings to the fictitious belief that by straining his foresight to the utmost he can control life. Consequently he avoids taking any step of which he cannot visualize the effects in advance: his uppermost law is never to be caught off guard. For such a person free association means the utmost recklessness, since it is the very meaning of the process to allow everything to emerge without knowing in advance what will appear and whither it will lead. The difficulty is of another kind for a highly detached person who feels safe only when wearing a mask and who automatically wards off any intrusion into the precincts of his private life. Such a one lives in an ivory tower and feels threatened by any attempt to trespass into its vicinity. For him free association means an unbearable intrusion and a threat to his isolation.

And there is the person who lacks moral autonomy and does not dare to form his own judgments. He is not accustomed to think and feel and act on his own initiative but, like an insect extending its feelers to test out the situation, he automatically examines the environment for what is expected of him. His thoughts are good or right when approved by others, and bad or wrong when disapproved. He, too, feels threatened by the idea of expressing everything that comes into his mind, but in quite a different way from the others: knowing only how to respond, not how to express himself spontaneously, he feels at a loss. What does the analyst expect of him? Should he merely talk incessantly? Is the analyst interested in his dreams? Or in his sexual life? Is he expected to fall in love with the analyst? And what does the latter approve or disapprove of? For this person the idea of frank and spontaneous self-expression conjures up all these disquieting uncertainties, and also threatens an exposure to possible disapproval.

And, finally, a person caught within the traps of his own conflicts has become inert and has lost the capacity to feel himself as a moving force. He can proceed with an endeavor only when the initiative comes from the outside. He is quite willing to answer questions but feels lost when left to his own resources. Thus he is unable to associate freely because his capacity for spontaneous activity is inhibited. And this inability to associate may provoke in him a kind of panic if he is one to whom success in all things is a driving necessity, for he is likely then to regard his inhibition as a "failure."

These examples illustrate how for some persons the whole process of free association arouses fears or inhibitions. But even those who are capable of the process in general have in them one or another area that gives rise to anxiety if it is touched upon. Thus in the example of Clare, who on the whole was able to associate freely, anything approaching her repressed demands on life aroused anxiety at the beginning of her analysis.

Another difficulty lies in the fact that an unreserved expression of all feelings and thoughts is bound to lay bare traits that the person is ashamed of and that he is humiliated to report. As mentioned in the chapter on neurotic trends, the traits that are regarded as humiliating vary considerably. A person who is proud of his cynical pursuit of material interests will be bewildered and ashamed if he betrays idealistic propensities. A person who is proud of his angelic façade will be ashamed to betray signs of selfishness and inconsiderateness. And the same humiliation will occur when any pretense is uncovered.

Many of the patient's difficulties in expressing his thoughts and feelings are related to the analyst. Thus the person who is unable to associate freely—whether because it would threaten his defenses or because he has lost too much of his own initiative—is likely to transfer to the analyst his aversion to the process or his chagrin at failure, and react with an unconscious defiant obstruction. That his own development, his happiness, is at stake is practically forgotten. And even if the process does not give rise to hostility toward the analyst there is the further fact that fears concerning the analyst's attitude are always present to some degree. Will he understand? Will he condemn? Will he look down upon me or turn against me? Is he really concerned with my own best development, or does he want to mold me into his pattern? Will he feel hurt if I make personal remarks about him? Will he lose patience if I do not accept his suggestions?

It is this infinite variety of concerns and obstacles that makes unreserved frankness such an extremely difficult task. As a result, evasive tactics will inevitably occur. The patient will deliberately omit certain incidents. Certain factors will never occur to him in the analytical hour. Feelings will not be expressed because they are too fleeting. Details will be omitted because he considers them trivial. "Figuring out" will take the place of a free flow of thoughts. He will stick to a long-winded account of daily occurrences. There is almost no end to the ways in which he may consciously or unconsciously try to evade this requirement.

Thus, while it may sound like a simple task to say everything that comes to one's mind, its difficulties in reality are so great that it can be only approximately fulfilled. The bigger the obstacles in the way, the more unproductive will the person become. But the more he approximates it, the more transparent will he be to himself and to the analyst.

The second task confronting the patient in analysis is to face his problems squarely—to gain an insight into them by recognizing factors that were hitherto unconscious. This is not only an intellectual process, however, as the word "recognize" might suggest; as emphasized in analytical literature since Ferenczi and Rank, it is both an intellectual and an emotional experience. If I may use a slang expression, it means gaining information about ourselves which we feel in our "guts."

The insight may be a recognition of an entirely repressed factor, such as the discovery made by a compulsively modest or benevolent person that actually he has a diffuse contempt for people. It may be a recognition that a drive which is at the level of awareness has an extent, intensity, and quality that were never dreamed of: a person may know that he is ambitious, for instance, but never have suspected before that his ambition is an all-devouring passion determining his life and containing the destructive element of wanting a vindictive triumph over others. Or the insight may be a finding that certain seemingly unconnected factors are closely interrelated. A person may have known that he has certain grandiose expectations as to his significance and his achievements in life, and have been aware also that he has a melancholy outlook and a general foreboding that he will succumb to some pending disaster within a brief span, but never have suspected that either attitude represents a problem or that the two have any connection. In this case his insight might reveal to him that his urge to be admired for his unique value is so rigid that he feels a deep indignation at its nonfulfillment and therefore devalues life itself: like an inveterate aristocrat who is faced with the necessity of stooping to a lower standard of living, he would rather stop living than be satisfied with less than he feels entitled to expect. Thus his preoccupation with impending disaster would actually represent an underlying wish to die, partly as a spiteful gesture toward life for not having measured up to his expectations.

It is impossible to say in general terms what it means to a patient to obtain an insight into his problems, just as it would be impossible to say what it means to a person to be exposed to sunshine. Sunshine may kill him or save his life, it may be fatiguing or refreshing, its effect depending on its intensity and also on his own condition. Similarly, an insight may be extremely painful or it may bring an immediate relief. Here we are on much the same ground as was covered above in the discussion of the therapeutic value of the various steps in analysis, but it will do no harm to recapitulate those remarks for this slightly different context.

There are several reasons why an insight may produce relief. To begin with the least important consideration, it is often a gratifying intellectual experience merely to

112

learn the reasons for some phenomenon not hitherto understood; in any situation in life it is likely to be a relief merely to recognize the truth. This consideration applies not only to elucidations of present peculiarities but also to memories of hitherto forgotten childhood experiences, if such memories help one to understand precisely what factors influenced one's development at the start.

More important is the fact that an insight may reveal to a person his own true feelings by showing him the speciousness of his former attitude. When he becomes free to express the anger, irritation, contempt, fear, or whatever it was that was hitherto repressed, an active and alive feeling has replaced a paralyzing inhibition and a step is taken toward finding himself. The inadvertent laughter that frequently occurs at such discoveries reveals the feeling of liberation. This may hold true even if the finding itself is far from agreeable, even if the person recognizes, for instance, that all his life he has merely tried to "get by" or has tried to hurt and dominate others. In addition to producing this increase in self-feeling, in aliveness, in activity, the insight may remove the tensions generated by his former necessity to check his true feelings: by increasing the forces that were needed for repression it may increase the amount of available energies.

Finally, closely related to the liberation of energies, the lifting of a repression frees the way for action. As long as a striving or feeling is repressed the person is caught in a blind alley. As long as he is entirely una-

113

ware of a hostility to others, for example, and knows only that he feels awkward with people, he is helpless to do anything about his hostility; there is no possibility of understanding the reasons for it or of discovering when it is justified or of diminishing or removing it. But if the repression is lifted and he feels the hostility as such, then and only then can he take a good look at it and proceed to discover the vulnerable spots in himself which produced it and to which he has been as blind as to the hostility itself. By thus opening up the possibility of eventually changing something about the disturbing factors, the insight is likely to produce considerable relief. Even if immediate change is difficult there is the vision of a future way out of the distress. This holds true even though the initial reaction may be one of hurt or fright. Clare's insight into the fact that she had excessive wishes and demands for herself provoked a panic in her at first, because it shook the compulsive modesty which was one of the pillars supporting her feeling of security. But as soon as the acute anxiety subsided it gave her relief, for it represented the possibility of a liberation from the shackles that had tied her hand and foot.

But the first reaction to an insight may be one of pain rather than relief. As discussed in a previous chapter, there are two principal kinds of negative responses to an insight. One is to feel it only as a threat; the other is to react in discouragement and hopelessness. Different though they appear, these two responses are essentially merely variations in degree. They are both determined by the fact that the person is not, or not yet, able and willing to give up certain fundamental claims on life. Which claims they are depends, of course, on his neurotic trends.

It is because of the compulsive nature of these trends that the claims are so rigid and so hard to relinquish. One who is obsessed by a craving for power, for instance, can do without comfort, pleasures, women, friends, everything that usually makes life desirable, but power he must have. As long as he is determined not to relinquish this claim, any questioning of its value can only irritate or frighten him. Such fright reactions are produced not only by insights disproving the feasibility of his particular striving but also by those revealing that its pursuit prevents him from attaining other objectives that are also important to him, or from overcoming painful handicaps and sufferings. Or, to take other examples, one who suffers from his isolation and his awkwardness in contacts with others, but is still basically unwilling to leave his ivory tower, must react with anxiety to any insight showing him that he cannot possibly attain the one objective—less isolation—without abandoning the other—his ivory tower. As long as a person basically refuses to relinquish his compulsive belief that he can master life through the sheer force of his will, any insight indicating the fictitious nature of that belief must arouse anxiety, because it makes him feel as if the ground on which he stands is pulled away from under him.

The anxiety produced by such insights is the person's

response to a dawning vision that he must eventually change something in his foundations *if* he wants to become free. But the factors that must be changed are still deeply entrenched, are still vitally important to him as a means of coping with himself and others. He is therefore afraid to change, and the insight produces not relief but panic.

And if he feels deep down that such a change, though indispensable for his liberation, is entirely out of the question, he will react with a feeling of hopelessness rather than fright. In his conscious mind this feeling is often overshadowed by a deep anger toward the analyst. He feels that the analyst is being pointlessly cruel in leading him to such insights when he cannot do anything about them anyhow. This reaction is understandable because none of us is willing to endure hurts and hardships if they do not ultimately serve some purpose we affirm.

A negative reaction to an insight is not necessarily the last word in the matter. Sometimes, in fact, it is of relatively short duration and quickly changes to relief. I need not elaborate here the factors that determine whether a person's attitude toward a particular insight can change through further psychoanalytic work. It is sufficient to say that a change is within the range of possibility.

Reactions to findings about ourselves cannot be fully understood, however, by thus cataloguing them as producing relief or fear or hopelessness. No matter what immediate reaction is provoked, an insight always means

116

a challenge to the existing equilibrium. A person driven by compulsive needs has functioned badly. He has pursued certain goals at great expense to his genuine wishes. He is inhibited in many ways. He is vulnerable in large and diffuse areas. The necessity to combat repressed fears and hostilities saps his energy. He is alienated from himself and others. But notwithstanding all these defects in his psychic machinery the forces operating within him still constitute an organic structure within which each factor is interrelated with the others. In consequence, no factor can be changed without influencing the whole organism. Strictly speaking there is no such thing as an isolated insight. Naturally it often happens that a person will stop at one or another point. He may be satisfied with the result attained, he may be discouraged, he may actively resist going farther. But in principle every insight gained, no matter how small in itself, opens up new problems because of its interrelation with other psychic factors, and thereby carries dynamite with which the whole equilibrium can be shaken. The more rigid the neurotic system, the less can any modification be tolerated. And the more closely an insight touches upon the foundations, the more anxiety will it arouse. "Resistance," as I shall elaborate later on, ultimately springs from the need to maintain the *status quo*.

The third task awaiting the patient is to change those factors within himself which interfere with his best development. This does not mean only a gross modification in action or behavior, such as gaining or regaining

117

the capacity for public performances, for creative work, for co-operation, for sexual potency, or losing phobias or tendencies toward depression. These changes will automatically take place in a successful analysis. They are not primary changes, however, but result from less visible changes within the personality, such as gaining a more realistic attitude toward oneself instead of wavering between self-aggrandizement and self-degradation, gaining a spirit of activity, assertion, and courage instead of inertia and fears, becoming able to plan instead of drifting, finding the center of gravity within oneself instead of hanging on to others with excessive expectations and excessive accusations, gaining greater friendliness and understanding for people instead of harboring a defensive diffuse hostility. If changes like these take place external changes in overt activities or symptoms are bound to follow, and to a corresponding degree.

Many changes that go on within the personality do not constitute a special problem. Thus an insight may in itself constitute a change, if it is a real emotional experience. One might say that nothing has changed if an insight is gained, for example, into a hostility hitherto repressed: the hostility is still there, and only the awareness of it is different. This is true only in a mechanistic sense. Actually it makes an enormous difference if the person who had known only that he was stilted, fatigued, or diffusely irritated recognizes the concrete hostility which, through its very repression, had generated these disturbances. As already discussed, he may feel like another human being in such a moment of discovery. And unless he manages to discard the recognition immediately it is bound to influence his relations with other people; it will arouse a feeling of surprise at himself, stimulate an incentive to investigate the meaning of the hostility, remove his feeling of helplessness in the face of something unknown, and make him feel more alive.

There are also changes that occur automatically as an indirect result of an insight. The patient's compulsive needs will be diminished as soon as any source of anxiety is diminished. As soon as a repressed feeling of humiliation is seen and understood, a greater friendliness will result automatically, even though the desirability of friendliness has not been touched upon. If a fear of failure is recognized and lessened, the person will spontaneously become more active and take risks that he hitherto unconsciously avoided.

Thus far, insight and change appear to coincide, and it might seem unnecessary to present these two processes as separate tasks. But there are situations during analysis—as there are in life itself—when despite an insight one may fight tooth and nail against changing. Some of these situations have already been discussed. They may be generalized by saying that when a patient recognizes that he must renounce or modify his compulsive claims on life, if he wants to have his energies free for his proper development, a hard fight may begin in which he uses his last resources to disprove the necessity or the possibility of change.

Another situation in which insight and change may be quite distinct arises when the analysis has led the person face to face with a conflict in which a decision must be made. Not all conflicts uncovered in psychoanalysis are of this nature. If contradictory drives are recognized between, for instance, having to control others and having to comply with their expectations, there is no question of deciding between the two tendencies. Both must be analyzed, and when the person has found a better relation to himself and others both will disappear or be considerably modified. It is a different matter, however, if a hitherto unconscious conflict emerges between material self-interest and ideals. The issue may have been befogged in various ways: the cynical attitude may have been conscious while the ideals were repressed, or consciously refuted if they sometimes penetrated to the surface; or the wish for material advantages (money, prestige) may have been repressed while consciously the ideals were rigidly adhered to; or there may have been a continual crisscrossing between taking ideals in a cynical or in a serious way. But when such a conflict comes out in the open it is not enough to see it and to understand its ramifications. After a thorough clarification of all the problems involved the patient must eventually take a stand. He must make up his mind whether and to what extent he wants to take his ideals seriously, and what space he will allot to material interests. Here, then, is one of the occasions when a patient may hesitate to take the step from insight to a revision of his attitudes.

It is certainly true, however, that the three tasks with which a patient is confronted are closely interrelated. His complete self-expression prepares the way for the insights, and the insights bring about or prepare for the change. Each step influences the others. The more he shrinks back from gaining a certain insight, the more his free associations will be impeded. The more he resists a certain change, the more he will fight an insight. The goal, however, is change. The high value attributed to self-recognition is not for the sake of insight alone, but for the sake of insight as a means of revising, modifying, controlling the feelings, strivings, and attitudes.

The patient's attitude toward changing often goes through various steps. Frequently he starts treatment with unadmitted expectations of a magical cure, which usually means a hope that all his disturbances will vanish without his having to change anything or even without having to work actively at himself. Consequently he endows the analyst with magical powers and tends to admire him blindly. Then, when he realizes that this hope cannot be fulfilled, he tends to withdraw the previous "confidence" altogether. He argues that if the analyst is a simple human being like himself what good can he do him? More important, his own feeling of hopelessness about doing anything actively with himself comes to the surface. Only when and if his energies can be liberated for active and spontaneous work can he finally regard his development as his own job, and the analyst as someone who merely lends him a helping hand.

The tasks with which the patient in analysis is confronted are replete with difficulties and with benefits. To express oneself with utter frankness is hard, but it is also a blessing. And the same can be said about gaining

ity, defiance, compliance, suspicion, confidence, assertiveness, timidity, ruthlessness, sensitivity. In the mere process of listening to the patient he will, without direct effort, gain many general impressions: whether the patient is able to let himself go or is tense and constrained; whether he talks in a systematic, controlled fashion or is jumpy and scattered; whether he presents abstract generalities or concrete details; whether he is circumstantial or to the point; whether he talks spontaneously or leaves the initiative to the analyst; whether he is conventional or expresses what he really thinks and feels.

In his more specific observations the analyst learns, first, from what the patient tells him about his experiences, past and present, his relationships with himself and others, his plans, his wishes, his fears, his thoughts. Second, he learns from observing the patient's behavior in his office, for each patient reacts differently to arrangements concerning fees, time, lying down, and other objective aspects of analysis. And each patient reacts differently to the fact that he is being analyzed. One patient regards analysis as an interesting intellectual process but refutes the idea that he really needs it; another treats it as a humiliating secret; while a third is proud of it as a special privilege. Moreover, patients exhibit an endless variety of attitudes toward the analyst himself, with as many individual shades as exist otherwise in human relationships. Finally, patients show innumerable subtle and gross vacillations in their reactions, and these vacillations themselves are revealing. These two sources of information—the patient's communications about himself and the observation of his actual behavior—complement each other just as they do in any relationship. Even if we know a great deal about a person's history and all his present ways of dealing with friends, women, business, politics, our picture of him becomes far more clear and complete if we meet him personally and see him in action. Both sources are indispensable; one is no less important than the other.

Like any other observation, that of the analyst is tinged by the nature of his interest. A saleswoman will heed other qualities in a customer than a social worker will in a client applying for help. An employer interviewing a prospective employee will focus on questions of initiative, adaptability, reliability, while a minister talking to a parishioner will be more interested in questions of moral behavior and religious belief. The analyst's interest does not focus upon one part of the patient, not even upon the disturbed part, but necessarily embraces the whole personality. Since he wants to understand its entire structure, and since he does not know offhand what may be more relevant and what less, his attention must absorb as many factors as possible.

The specific analytical observations derive from the analyst's purpose of recognizing and understanding the patient's unconscious motivations. This is their essential difference from general observations. In the latter, too, we may sense certain undercurrents, but such impressions remain more or less tentative and even unformulated; also, we do not bother as a rule to distinguish whether they are determined by psychic factors of our own or by those of the observed person. The analyst's specific observations, however, are an indispensable part of the analytic process. They constitute a systematic study of unconscious forces as revealed in the patient's free associations. To these the analyst listens attentively, trying not to select any one element prematurely but to pay an even interest to every detail.

Some of the analyst's observations will fall in line immediately. Just as one discerns in a foggy landscape the dim outline of a house or a tree, the analyst will have no difficulty in quickly recognizing one or another general character trait. But for the most part his observations are only a maze of seemingly unconnected items. How, then, does he arrive at an understanding?

In some ways his work might be compared with that of the detective in mystery stories. It is worth emphasizing, however, that whereas the detective wants to discover the criminal the analyst does not want to find out what is bad in the patient, but attempts to understand him as a whole, good and bad. Also, he deals not with several people, all under suspicion, but with a multitude of driving forces in one person, all under suspicion not of being bad but of being disturbing. Through concentrated and intelligent observation of every detail he gathers his clues, sees a possible connection here and there, and forms a tentative picture; he is not too easily convinced of his solution, but tests it over and over again to see whether it really embraces all factors. In mystery stories there will be some people working with the de-

126

tective, some only apparently doing so and secretly ob-structing his work, some definitely wanting to hide and becoming aggressive if they feel threatened. Similarly, in analysis part of the patient co-operates—this is an in-dispensable condition—another part expects the analyst to do all the work and still another uses all its energies to hide or mislead and becomes panicky and hostile when threatened with discovery.

It is mainly from the patient's free associations, as described in the previous chapter, that the analyst de-rives his understanding of unconscious motivations and reactions. The patient is not usually aware of the impli-cations of what he presents. Therefore the analyst, in order to form a coherent picture out of the multitude of discrepant elements presented to him, must not only listen to the manifest content but also try to understand what the patient really wants to express. He tries to grasp the red thread that passes through the apparently amor-phous mass of material. If too many unknown quantities are involved he sometimes fails in this endeavor. Some-times the context almost speaks for itself. The following examples are selected for their simplicity.

A patient tells me that he had a bad night and that he feels more depressed than ever. His secretary has had an attack of influenza, and this not only disturbs his busi-ness arrangements but also upsets him because of his fear of infection. He talks then about the frightful injustice done to small European countries. Then he thinks of a physician who annoyed him by failing to give him clear information about the contents of a drug. Then a tailor comes up in his mind who had not delivered a coat as promised.

The main theme is annoyance at untoward events. The egocentric nature of the grievances is shown by his enumerating the secretary's illness in one line with the unreliability of the tailor, as if both were personal offenses against him. The fact that the secretary's flu has rearoused his fear of infection does not lead him to think that he should try to overcome this fear. He expects, instead, that the world should be so arranged as not to arouse his fears. The world should attend to his needs. Here the theme of injustice comes in: it is unfair that others do not heed his expectations. Since he is afraid of infection nobody in his environment should fall ill. Thus others become responsible for his difficulties. He is as helpless against such influences as small European countries are against invasion (actually he is helpless in the clutches of his own expectations). The association concerning the doctor also acquires a special meaning in this context. It, too, implies expectations not complied with, and in addition it refers to his grievance against me for not offering him a clear solution of his problems, instead of groping around and expecting his co-operative activity.

Another simple example. A young girl tells me that she had an attack of heartpounding when shopping. Her heart was not strong, but she did not see why shopping should affect it since she could dance for hours without harm. Nor could she see any psychic reasons for the heartpounding. She had bought a superbly beautiful blouse for her older sister as a birthday gift, and was delighted to do so. She anticipated with pleasure how much the sister would enjoy and admire the gift. Actually, she had spent her last penny on it. She was short of money because she had straightened out all her debts, or at any rate had made arrangements by which she could pay them off in several months. This she said with distinct self-admiration. The blouse was so beautiful that she would have liked to have it herself. Then, after having apparently dropped the subject, a number of grievances against the sister appeared. She complained bitterly about how the sister interfered with her, how she made nonsensical reproaches. These grievances were intermingled with derogatory remarks which made the sister appear quite inferior to the patient.

Even at first sight this unpremeditated sequence of emotions indicates conflicting feelings toward the sister: a wish to win her love, and, on the other hand, resentment. When shopping, this conflict was accentuated. The loving side asserted itself in the purchase of the present; the resentment had to be suppressed for the time being and thus clamored all the louder for its share. The result was the heartpounding. Such clashes of contradictory feelings will not always elicit anxiety. Usually one of the incompatible feelings is repressed, or both join in some compromise solution. Here, as the associations show, no side of the conflict was altogether repressed. Instead, love and resentment, both on a conscious level, were placed on a seesaw. When the one feeling went up, in awareness, the other went down.

On closer scrutiny the associations disclosed more details. The theme of self-admiration, blatant in the first series, reappears implicitly in the second. The derogatory remarks about the sister not only express diffuse hostility but serve to make the patient's own light outshine the sister's. The tendency to put herself above the sister is evident throughout the associations, in the fact that she continually, even though inadvertently, contrasted her own generosity and sacrificing love with the sister's bad behavior. This close connection between self-admiration and rivalry with the sister suggests the possibility that the need to be superior to the sister was an essential factor in the development and maintenance of the self-admiration. This assumption also sheds another light on the conflict that occurred in the store. The impulse to buy the expensive blouse represented not only, as it were, a heroic determination to resolve the conflict but also a wish to establish her own supremacy over the sister, partly by winning her admiration, partly by showing herself the more loving, sacrificing, forgiving. On the other hand, by giving to the sister a more beautiful blouse than she had, she actually placed her in a "superior" position. In order to understand the importance of this point, it should be mentioned that the question of who was better dressed played a significant role in the battle of rivalry; the patient, for instance, had often appropriated the sister's dresses.

In these examples the process of understanding is relatively simple, but they make it clear that no observations should be regarded as unimportant. Just as the patient should express without reserve everything that comes to his mind, the analyst should regard every detail as potentially meaningful. He should not discard offhand any remark as irrelevant but should take seriously every single observation, without exception.

Furthermore, he should constantly ask himself why this particular feeling or thought of the patient comes up just now. What does it mean in this specific context? A friendly feeling toward the analyst, for instance, may in one context indicate genuine gratitude for help and understanding; in another it may connote the patient's increased need for affection because in the preceding hour the tackling of a new problem aroused anxiety; in a third it may be the expression of a desire to own the analyst body and soul because a conflict has been uncovered which the patient hopes that "love" will solve. In the example cited in the previous chapter the analyst was compared to a robber or a racketeer, not because of a permanent grievance against him, but for the specific reason that the patient's pride had been hurt in the previous hour. The association concerning the injustice done to European countries would have a different meaning in another context—sympathy with the oppressed, for example. It was only in conjunction with the patient's annoyance at the secretary's illness and his other associations that this remark revealed how intensely he felt it unfair that his expectations were not met. A failure to examine an association's exact connections with preceding and succeeding associations, and with preceding experiences, may not only lead to wrong interpretations but also deprive the analyst of an opportunity to learn something about the patient's reactions to a specific occurrence.

The chain of associations that reveals a connection need not be a long one. Sometimes a sequence of only two remarks opens up a path for understanding, provided the second is not a brainchild but is born spontaneously. A patient, for instance, came to analysis feeling tired and uneasy, and his first associations were unproductive. He had been drinking the night before. I asked him whether he had a hangover, which he denied. The last hour had been very productive for it had brought to light the fact that he was afraid of taking responsibility because he was terrified of possible failure. Thus I asked him whether he wanted to rest on his laurels. At this a memory emerged of his mother dragging him through museums and of his boredom and annoyance at the experience. There was only this one association, but it was revealing. It was partly a response to my remark about his resting on his laurels. I was just as bad as the mother pushing him from one problem to another. (This reaction was characteristic of him because he was hypersensitive to anything resembling coercion, though at the same time his own initiative for tackling problems was inhibited.) Having become aware of his annoyance with me and of his active reluctance to go on, he then felt free to feel and express another sentiment. Its essence was that psychoanalysis was worse than the situation in the museum because it meant being dragged on to see one failure after another. With this association he unintentionally resumed the thread of the preceding hour, which had revealed his hypersensitivity to failure. It meant an elaboration of the previous findings for it showed that for him any factor in his personality which prevented him from functioning smoothly and effectively meant a "failure." He thereby revealed one of his basic resistances to psychoanalysis.

The same patient came another time feeling depressed. He had met a friend the night before who told him about his climbing of a Swiss mountain, the Piz Palü. The report had awakened the memory of a time when he was in Switzerland and could not climb this mountain because it was befogged during the days he had at his disposal. He had been furious at that time, and the night before he had felt the old rage rising again. He lay awake for hours evolving plans how he could still assert his wish, how he could overcome all obstacles of war, money, time. Even after he fell asleep his mind fought against the obstacles in his way, and he awoke depressed. During the analysis an apparently irrelevant picture came up in his mind of the outskirts of a Midwestern town, which for him was the epitome of the drab and desolate. This mental image expressed his feelings about life at that moment. But what was the connection? That life was desolate if he could not climb the Piz Palü? It is true that when he was in Switzerland he had set his heart upon climbing the mountain, but the frustration of this special wish could hardly be the explanation. Mountain climbing was no passion of his; the incident had occurred years ago and he had since forgotten about it. Apparently, then, it was not the Piz Palü that was bothering him.

133

When he calmed down he realized that he would not even care to climb it now. The revival of that Swiss experience meant something much more incisive. It had disturbed an illusory belief that if he set his will on achieving something he should be able to do it. Any unsurpassable obstacle meant to him a frustration of his will, even if it was so much out of his command as a fog in the mountains. The associations concerning the desolate outskirts of a Midwestern town indicated the enormous significance he attached to his belief in the sheer force of will. It meant that life was not worth living if he must relinquish this belief.

Repetitive themes or sequences in the material presented by the patient are particularly helpful for understanding. If the associations end always with implicit evidence that the patient has superior intelligence or rationality, or is in general a remarkable person, the analyst will understand that his belief in his possession of these qualities is of paramount emotional value to him. A patient who misses no opportunity to demonstrate how analysis has harmed him will lead the analyst to different hypotheses from those suggested by a patient who misses no opportunity to emphasize his improvement. In the former instance if the demonstrations of impairment coincide with repeated reports of being unfairly treated, injured, or victimized, the analyst will begin to watch for those factors within the patient that explain why he experiences a large proportion of life in exactly this way, and also for the consequences entailed by this attitude. Repetitive themes, since they reveal certain typical reactions, also provide a clue for under-standing why the patient's experiences often follow a certain stereotyped pattern; for example, why he fre-quently starts on an enterprise with enthusiasm and drops it soon after, or why he frequently encounters similar disappointments with friends or lovers.

The analyst will find valuable clues also in the patient's contradictions, of which as many are bound to appear as are present in the patient's structure. The same holds true of exaggerations, such as reactions of violence, grati-tude, shame, suspicion, apparently disproportionate to the provocation. Such a surplus of affect always signal-izes a hidden problem, and it leads the analyst to look for the emotional significance that the provocation has for the patient.

Dreams and fantasies are also of eminent importance as a means toward understanding. Since they are a rela-tively direct expression of unconscious feelings and striv-ings they may open up avenues for understanding that are otherwise hardly visible. Some dreams are rather transparent; as a rule, however, they speak a cryptic lan-guage that can be understood only with the assistance of free associations.

The particular point at which the patient turns from co-operation to defensive maneuvers of one kind or another furnishes another help for understanding. As the analyst gradually discovers the reasons for these resist-ances he gains increasing understanding of the patient's peculiarities. Sometimes the fact that a patient stalls or fights, and the immediate reason why he does so, are

135

SELF-ANALYSIS

transparent. More often astute observation is necessary to detect that a blockage exists, and the help of the patient's free associations is necessary to understand the reasons for it. If the analyst succeeds in understanding the resistance he will gain an increased knowledge as to the precise factors that hurt or frighten the patient and the precise nature of the reaction they produce.

Similarly illuminating are the themes that the patient omits, or deserts quickly if he touches upon them. The analyst will have an important clue if, for example, the patient rigidly avoids expressing any critical thoughts concerning the analyst though he is otherwise over-exacting and overcritical. Another example of this kind would be a patient's failure to tell a specific incident which had occurred the previous day and had upset him.

All these clues help the analyst to obtain gradually a coherent picture of the patient's life, past and present, and of the forces operating in his personality. But they also help toward an understanding of the factors operating in the patient's relationship to the analyst and the analytical situation. For several reasons it is important to understand this relationship as accurately as possible. For one thing, it would block the analysis entirely if, for instance, a hidden resentment toward the analyst remained under cover. With the best will in the world a patient cannot express himself freely and spontaneously if he has an unsolved resentment in his heart toward the person to whom he reveals himself. Second, since the patient cannot feel and react differently toward the analyst from the way he does toward other people, he unconsciously displays in analysis the same irrational emotional factors, the same strivings and reactions, that he displays in other relationships. Thus the co-operative study of these factors makes it possible for the analyst to understand the patient's disturbances in his human relationships in general, and these, as we have seen, are the crucial issue in the whole neurosis.

The clues that may help toward a gradual understanding of the patient's structure are, in fact, practically infinite. But it is important to mention that the analyst makes use of the clues not only by means of precise reasoning but also, as it were, intuitively. In other words, he cannot always precisely explain how he arrives at his tentative assumption. In my own work, for example, I have arrived sometimes at an understanding through free associations of my own. While listening to a patient some incident may emerge in my mind that the patient has told me long ago, without my knowing offhand what bearing it has on the present situation. Or a finding regarding another patient may occur to me. I have learned never to discard these associations, and they have often proved helpful when they were seriously examined.

When the analyst has recognized some possible connection, when he has gained an impression as to the unconscious factors that may be operating in a certain context, he will tell the patient his interpretation—if he sees fit to do so. Since this is no discourse on psychoanalytic technique, and since the art of timing and meting out interpretations is irrelevant in self-analysis, it may suffice here to say that the analyst will offer an interpretation if he thinks the patient can stand it and can utilize it.

Interpretations are suggestions as to possible meanings. They are by nature more or less tentative, and the patient's reactions to them vary. If an interpretation is essentially right it may strike home and stimulate associations showing its further implications. Or the patient may test it out and gradually qualify it. Even when it is only partly right it may thus give rise to new trends of thought, provided the patient is co-operating. But an interpretation may also provoke anxiety or defensive reactions. Here the discussion in the preceding chapter, concerning the patient's reaction to insights, is relevant. Whatever the reactions are, the analyst's task is to understand them and learn from them.

Psychoanalysis in its very essence is co-operative work, both patient and analyst bent on understanding the patient's difficulties. The latter tries to lay himself open to the analyst and, as we have seen, the analyst observes, tries to understand, and, if appropriate, conveys his interpretation to the patient. He then makes suggestions as to possible meanings and both try to test out the validity of the suggestions. They try to recognize, for instance, whether an interpretation is right only for the present context or is of general importance, whether it has to be qualified or is valid only under certain conditions. And as long as such a co-operative spirit prevails it is comparatively easy for the analyst to understand the patient and to convey to him his findings.

The real difficulties arise when, in technical terms,

138

the patient develops a "resistance." Then, in tangible or intangible ways, he refuses to co-operate. He is late or forgets the appointment. He wants to take some days or weeks off. He loses interest in the common work and mainly wants the analyst's love and friendship. His associations become shallow, unproductive, and evasive. Instead of examining suggestions made by the analyst, he resents them and feels attacked, hurt, misunderstood, humiliated. He may reject every attempt to help with a rigid feeling of hopelessness and futility. Fundamentally the reason for this impasse is that certain insights are not acceptable to the patient; they are too painful, too frightening, and they undermine illusions that he cherishes and is incapable of relinquishing. Therefore he fights them off in one way or another, though he does not know that he is attempting to ward off painful insights: all he knows, or thinks he knows, is that he is misunderstood or humiliated or that the work is futile.

Up to this point the analyst, on the whole, has followed the patient. There is a certain amount of implicit guidance, of course, in each suggestion of a possible lead—a new slant offered by an interpretation, a question raised, a doubt expressed. But for the most part the initiative lies with the patient. When a resistance has developed, however, interpretative work and implicit guidance may be insufficient, and then the analyst must definitely take the lead. In these periods his task is, first, to recognize the resistance as such, and, second, to help the patient to recognize it. And he must not only help him to see that he is engaged in a defensive battle but also find out, with or without the patient's help, what it is that the latter is warding off. He does so by going back in his mind over the previous sessions and trying to discover what may have struck the patient before the session in which the resistance started.

It is sometimes easy to do this, but it may be extremely difficult. The beginning of the resistance may have been unnoticeable. The analyst may not yet be aware of the patient's vulnerable spots. But if the analyst can recognize the presence of a resistance, and can succeed in convincing the patient that one is operating, the source can often be discovered through common search. The immediate gain from this discovery is that the way is cleared for further work, but an understanding of the sources of a resistance also provides the analyst with significant information concerning the factors the patient wants to keep under cover.

The analyst's active guidance is likely to be particularly necessary when the patient has arrived at an insight that has far-reaching implications—for example, when he has succeeded in seeing a neurotic trend and in recognizing in it a driving force of primary order. This could be a time of harvest, a time in which many previous findings might fall in line and further ramifications might become apparent. What frequently happens instead is that at this very point, for reasons presented in the third chapter, the patient develops a resistance and tries to get away with as little as possible. He may do so in various ways. He may automatically search for and express some ready-at-hand explanation. Or he may in a more or less subtle way disparage the significance of the finding. He may respond with good resolutions to control the trend by sheer will, a course which recalls the paving of the road to hell. Finally, he may prematurely raise the question why the trend has obtained such a hold on him, delving into his childhood and at best bringing forth relevant data contributing to the understanding of origins, for he is actually using this dive into the past as a means of escaping from the realization of what the discovered trend means for his actual life.

These efforts to rush away from an important insight as quickly as possible are understandable. It is difficult for a person to face the fact that he has put all his energies into the pursuit of a phantom. More important, such an insight confronts him with the necessity for radical change. It is only natural that he should tend to close his eyes to a necessity so disturbing to his whole equilibrium. But the fact remains that through this hasty retreat he prevents the insight from "sinking in" and thereby deprives himself of the benefits it might mean for him. Here the help the analyst can give is to take the lead, revealing to the patient his recoiling tactics and also encouraging him to work through in great detail all the consequences the trend has for his life. As mentioned before, a trend can be coped with only if its extent and intensity and implications are fully confronted.

Another point at which a resistance may necessitate active guidance from the analyst occurs when the patient unconsciously shirks a square recognition that he is caught in a conflict of opposing drives. Here again his tendency to maintain the *status quo* may block all progress. His associations may represent only a futile shuttling between one aspect of the conflict and another. He may talk about his need to force others into helping him by arousing pity, and soon after about his pride preventing him from accepting any help. As soon as the analyst comments on the one aspect he will shuttle to the other. This unconscious strategy may be difficult to recognize because in pursuing it the patient may bring forth valuable material here and there. Nevertheless, it is the analyst's task to recognize such evasive maneuvers and to direct the patient's activity toward a square recognition of the existing conflict.

Also in the later phases of analysis it is sometimes necessary for the analyst to assume the lead in dealing with a resistance. He may be struck by a realization that despite much work done, much insight gained, nothing changes in the patient. In such cases he must desert his role as interpreter and confront the patient openly with the discrepancy between insight and change, possibly raising the question as to unconscious reservations that the patient may have which prevent him from letting any insight really touch him.

Thus far the analyst's work is of an intellectual character: he puts his knowledge into the service of the patient. But his help extends beyond what he can give on the basis of his specific competence, even if he is not aware of offering more than his technical skill.

In the first place, by his very presence, he gives the

142

patient a unique opportunity to become aware of his behavior toward people. In other relationships the patient is likely to focus his thinking primarily on the peculiarities of others, their injustice, their selfishness, their defiance, their unfairness, their unreliability, their hostility; even if he is aware of his own reactions he is inclined to regard them as provoked by the others. In analysis, however, this particular personal complication is almost entirely absent, not only because the analyst has been analyzed, and continues to analyze himself, but also because his life is not entangled with the patient's life. This detachment isolates the patient's peculiarities from the befogging circumstances that ordinarily surround them.

And in the second place, by his friendly interest, the analyst gives the patient a good deal of what may be called general human help. To some extent this is inseparable from the intellectual help. Thus the simple fact that the analyst wants to understand the patient implies that he takes him seriously. This in itself is an emotional support of primary importance, especially at those times when the patient is harassed by emerging fears and doubts, when his frailties are exposed, his pride attacked, his illusions undermined, for the patient is often too alienated from himself to take himself seriously. This statement may sound implausible, because most neurotic persons have an inordinate sense of their own importance, either in regard to their unique potentialities or in regard to their unique needs. But to think of ourselves as all important is radically different from taking ourselves seriously. The former attitude derives from an inflated image of the self; the latter refers to the real self and its development. A neurotic person often rationalizes his lack of seriousness in terms of "unselfishness" or in a contention that it is ridiculous or presumptuous to give much thought to oneself. This fundamental disinterest in the self is one of the great difficulties in self-analysis, and, conversely, one of the great advantages of professional analysis is the fact that it means working with someone who through his own attitude inspires the courage to be on friendly terms with oneself.

This human support is particularly valuable when the patient is in the grip of an emerging anxiety. In such situations the analyst will rarely reassure the patient directly. But the fact that the anxiety is tackled as a concrete problem, which can be solved eventually, lessens the terror of the unknown, regardless of the content of the interpretation. Similarly, when the patient is discouraged and inclined to give up the struggle the analyst does more for him than merely interpreting: his very attempt to understand this attitude as the outcome of a conflict is a greater support to the patient than any patting on the back or any effort to encourage him in so many words.

There are also the times when those fictitious foundations upon which the patient has built up his pride become shaky, and he starts to doubt himself. It is good to lose harmful illusions about oneself. But we must not forget that in all neuroses solid self-confidence is greatly impaired. Fictitious notions of superiority substitute for it. But the patient, in the midst of his struggle, cannot distinguish between the two. To him an undermining of his inflated notions means a destruction of his faith in himself. He realizes that he is not as saintly, as loving, as powerful, as independent as he had believed, and he cannot accept himself bereft of glory. At that point he needs someone who does not lose faith in him, even though his own faith is gone.

In more general terms the human help that the analyst gives the patient is similar to what one friend might give to another: emotional support, encouragement, interest in his happiness. This may constitute the patient's first experience of the possibility of human understanding, the first time that another person has bothered to see that he is not simply a spiteful, suspicious, cynical, demanding, bluffing individual, but, with a clear recognition of such trends, still likes and respects him as a striving and struggling human being. And if the analyst has proved to be a reliable friend, this good experience may help the patient also to retrieve his faith in others.

Since our interest here is in the possibility of self-analysis it may be well to review these functions of the analyst and see to what extent they can be taken over by a patient working alone.

There is no doubt that the observations of a trained outsider will be more accurate than our observation of ourselves, particularly so since concerning ourselves we are far from impartial. Against this disadvantage, however, stands the fact, already discussed, that we are more familiar with ourselves than any outsider can be. Experience gained in psychoanalytic treatment shows beyond any doubt that patients can develop an amazing faculty of keen self-observation if they are bent on understanding their own problems.

In self-analysis understanding and interpreting are a single process. The expert, as a result of his experience, will catch the possible meaning and significance of observations more quickly than will a person working alone, just as a good mechanic will know more quickly what is wrong with a car. As a rule his understanding will also be more complete, for it will grasp more implications and will more readily recognize interrelations with factors already tackled. Here the patient's psychological knowledge will be of some help, though it certainly cannot substitute for the experience gained by working day in and day out at psychological problems. It is unquestionably possible for him, however, as the example presented in Chapter Eight will demonstrate, to grasp the meaning of his own observations. To be sure, he will probably proceed more slowly and less accurately, but it should be remembered that also in professional analysis the tempo of the process is mainly determined not by the analyst's capacity to understand but by the patient's capacity to accept the insights. Here it is well to remember a word of consolation that Freud has given to young analysts starting their work with patients. They should not be too much concerned, he pointed out, with their capacity to evaluate associations. The real difficulty in analysis is not that of intellectual understanding but that of dealing with the patient's resistances. I believe that this holds true for self-analysis as well.

Can a person overcome his own resistances? This is the real question upon the answer to which hinges the feasibility of self-analysis. Nevertheless, the comparison with pulling oneself up by one's bootstraps—which is bound to occur—seems unwarranted, because the fact remains that there is one part of the self which wants to go ahead. Whether the job can be done depends, of course, on the intensity of the resistances as well as on the strength of the incentive to overcome them. But the important question—and I shall not attempt to answer it until a later chapter—is to what extent it can be done rather than whether it can be done at all.

There remains the fact that the analyst is not merely an interpreting voice. He is a human being, and the human relationship between him and the patient is an important factor in the therapeutic process. Two aspects of this relationship were pointed out, the first being that it presents a unique and specific opportunity for the patient to study, by observing his behavior with the analyst, what his typical behavior is toward other people in general. This advantage can be fully replaced if he learns to watch himself in his customary relationships. The expectations, wishes, fears, vulnerabilities, and inhibitions that he displays in his work with the analyst are not essentially different from those he displays in his relations with friends, lover, wife, children, employer, colleagues, or servants. If he is seriously intent upon recognizing the ways in which his peculiarities enter into all these relationships, ample opportunities for self-scrutiny are provided him by the mere fact that he is a social being.

But whether he will make full use of these sources of information is, of course, another question. There is no doubt that he faces an arduous task when he attempts to estimate his own share in the tensions between himself and others—a task much more arduous than that in the analytical situation, where the analyst's personal equation is negligible, and it is therefore easier for him to see the difficulties that he himself produces. In ordinary relationships, where the others are replete with peculiarities of their own, he may tend, even if he has the most sincere intentions to observe himself objectively, to make them responsible for the difficulties or frictions that arise, and to regard himself as an innocent victim or, at best, as showing merely a justified reaction to their unreasonableness. In the latter case he will not necessarily be so unsubtle as to indulge in overt accusations; he may admit in an apparently rational manner that he has been irritable, sulky, unfaithful, even unjust, but secretly regard such attitudes as justified and adequate responses to the offenses given by the others. The more intolerable it is for him to face his own frailties—and also the more acute the disturbing factors that are introduced by the others —the greater is the danger that he will thus deprive himself of the benefit he could derive from recognizing his own share. And the danger is of exactly the same nature if he tends to exaggerate in the opposite direction by whitewashing the others and blackening himself.

148

There is another factor that makes it easier for a person to see his peculiarities in the course of his relationship with the analyst than in his association with others. His disturbing character traits—his diffidence, dependency, arrogance, vindictiveness, his tendencies to withdraw and freeze up at the slightest hurts, or whatever they may be—are always contrary to his best self-interest, not only because they render his associations with others less satisfactory but also because they make him dissatisfied with himself. This fact is often blurred, however, in his customary relations with others. He feels that he will gain something by staying dependent, by taking revenge, by triumphing over others, and therefore he is less willing to recognize what he is doing. The same traits displayed in analysis work so blatantly against his self-interest that he can scarcely fail to see their injurious character, and hence the urge to blindfold himself against them is considerably lessened.

But while it is not easy it is entirely within the range of possibility for a person to overcome the emotional difficulties involved in studying his behavior toward others. As will be seen in the example of self-analysis presented in Chapter Eight, Clare analyzed the intricate problem of her morbid dependency by scrutinizing her relationship with her lover. And she succeeded in spite of the fact that both the difficulties mentioned above were present to a high degree: the disturbances in the personality of her lover were at least as great as her own; and certainly she had a vital interest, from the viewpoint of her neurotic expectations and fears, not to recognize

CHAPTER SIX

Occasional Self-Analysis

To analyze oneself occasionally is comparatively easy and sometimes productive of immediate results. Essentially it is what every sincere person does when he tries to account for real motivations behind the way he feels or acts. Without knowing much, if anything, about psychoanalysis, a man who has fallen in love with a particularly attractive or wealthy girl could raise with himself the question whether vanity or money plays a part in his feeling. A man who has ignored his better judgment and given in to his wife or his colleagues in an argument could question in his own mind whether he yielded because he was convinced of the comparative insignificance of the subject at stake or because he was afraid of an ensuing fight. I suppose people have always examined themselves in this way. And many people do so who otherwise tend to reject psychoanalysis entirely.

151

The principal domain of occasional self-analysis is not the intricate involvements of the neurotic character structure, but the gross manifest symptom, the concrete and usually acute disturbance which either strikes one's curiosity or commands one's immediate attention because of its distressing character. Thus the examples reported in this chapter concern a functional headache, an acute attack of anxiety, a lawyer's fear of public performances, an acute functional stomach upset. But a startling dream, the forgetting of an appointment, or an inordinate irritation at a taxidriver's trivial cheating might just as well elicit a wish to understand oneself—or, more precisely, to discover the reasons responsible for that particular effect.

This latter distinction may seem hairsplitting, but actually it expresses an important difference between occasional grappling with a problem and systematic work at oneself. The goal of occasional self-analysis is to recognize those factors that provoke a concrete disturbance, and to remove them. The broader incentive, the wish to be better equipped to deal with life in general, may operate here too, but even if it plays some role it is restricted to the wish to be less handicapped by certain fears, headaches, or other inconveniences. This is in contrast to the much deeper and more positive desire to develop to the best of one's capacities.

As the examples will indicate, the disturbances that produce an attempt at examination may be acute or of long standing; they may result predominantly from actual difficulties inherent in a situation or they may be expressions of a chronic neurosis. Whether they yield to a short-cut approach or can be solved with more intensive work depends on factors that will be discussed later.

Compared with the preconditions for a systematic self-analysis, those for occasional analysis are moderate. It suffices to have some psychological knowledge, and this need not be book knowledge but may be gained from ordinary experience. The only indispensable requirement is a willingness to believe that unconscious factors may be sufficiently powerful to throw the whole personality out of gear. To put it negatively, it is necessary not to be too easily satisfied with ready-at-hand explanations for a disturbance. A man, for instance, who has become inordinately upset about being cheated out of a dime by a taxidriver should not be content to tell himself that after all no one likes to be cheated. A person suffering from an acute depression must be skeptical about explaining his state on the basis of world conditions. Habitual forgetting of appointments is not very well explained by saying that one is too busy to remember.

It is particularly easy to brush aside those symptoms that are not obviously psychic in character, such as headaches, stomach upsets, or fatigue. As a matter of fact, one can observe two opposite attitudes toward such disturbances, both equally extreme and one sided. The one consists in automatically ascribing headaches to weather conditions, fatigue to overwork, stomach upsets to spoiled food or gastric ulcers, without even considering the possibility that psychic factors are involved. This attitude may be assumed because of sheer ignorance, but also it is a

believe that the following examples will sufficiently de-
lineate the problems involved in occasional self-analysis.

John

John, a good-natured businessman, apparently happily
married for five years, suffered from diffuse inhibitions
and "inferiority feelings" and in recent years had developed occasional headaches without any detectable
physical basis. He had not been analyzed but he was fairly
familiar with the psychoanalytic way of thinking. Later
he came to me for analysis of a rather intricate character
neurosis, and his experience in working alone was one
of the factors that convinced him of the possible value
of psychoanalytic therapy.

When he started to analyze his headaches it was without intending to do so. He, his wife, and two friends
went to a musical comedy and he developed a headache
during the play. This struck him as queer because he
had felt well before going to the theater. At first, with
some irritation, he ascribed his headache to the fact that
the play was bad and the evening was a waste of time, but
he soon realized that after all one does not get headaches
from a bad play. Now that he thought about it, the play
was not so bad after all. But of course it was nothing compared with the play of Shaw's that he would have preferred. These last words stuck in his mind—he "would
have preferred." Here he felt a flash of anger and saw
the connection. He had been overruled when the choice
between the plays was up for discussion. It was not even
much of a discussion: he felt he should be a good sport,
and what did it matter anyhow. Apparently it had mat-

tered to him, however, and he had been deeply angry about being coerced. With that recognition the headache was gone. He realized also that this was not the first headache that originated in this way. There were bridge parties, for instance, which he hated to join but was persuaded to do so.

He was startled to discover this connection between repressed anger and headaches, but he gave it no further thought. A few days later, however, he woke up early, again with a splitting headache. He had attended a staff meeting of his organization the night before. They had been drinking afterward, and at first he accounted for the headache by telling himself that probably he had drunk too much. With that he turned on the other side and tried to fall asleep again, but he could not. A fly buzzing around his face irritated him. At first the irritation was barely noticeable, but it grew rapidly to full-blown anger. Then he recalled a dream or a dream fragment: he had squashed two bedbugs with a piece of blotting paper. The blotting paper had many holes. As a matter of fact, he remembered that the holes were all over the paper and formed a regular pattern.

This reminded him of tissue paper that he had folded as a child, for cutting out patterns. He was quite taken by their beauty. An incident emerged in which he had shown the tissue to his mother, expecting admiration, but she had paid only perfunctory attention. The blotting paper then reminded him of the staff meeting. There he had scribbled on paper because he felt bored. No, he had not merely scribbled; he had drawn small caricatures of the chairman and of his opponent. The word "opponent" struck him, because he had not consciously regarded that person as an opponent. A resolution had had to be voted on, about which he felt vaguely uneasy. But he saw no clear objection to it. Hence the objection he had raised was actually not to the point. It was weak and made no impression. Only now he realized that they had put something over on him, for the acceptance of the resolution meant a lot of tedious work for himself. They had been so clever that it had escaped him. At this point he suddenly laughed because he recognized the meaning of the bedbugs. The chairman and the opponent—they were bloodsuckers, as distasteful as bedbugs. Also, he was as afraid of bedbugs as he was of these exploiters. Well, he had taken revenge—at least in his dream. Again the headache vanished.

On three subsequent occasions he searched for a hidden anger as soon as the headache started, found the anger and then lost his headache. After that the headaches disappeared entirely.

In reviewing this experience one is struck at first by the lightness of the labor in comparison with the result attained. But miracles occur in psychoanalysis as seldom as anywhere else. Whether a symptom can be easily removed depends on its function in the whole structure. In this case the headaches had not assumed any further role, such as preventing John from doing things he was afraid of doing or resented doing, or serving as a means of demonstrating to others that they had given offense or inflicted injury, or serving as a basis for demanding special consideration. If headaches or any other symptoms have assumed important functions such as these, their cure will require long and penetrating work. One will then have to analyze all the needs they satisfy and they will probably not disappear until the work is practically finished. In John's case they had not assumed any such functions, and probably resulted merely from tension increased by the repressed anger.

The extent of John's accomplishment is diminished also by another consideration. It was a gain, certainly, to be rid of the headaches, but it seems to me that we are inclined to overrate the significance of such gross, tangible symptoms and to underrate the importance of less tangible psychic disturbances, such as, in this case, John's alienation from his own wishes and opinions and his inhibition toward self-assertion. In these disturbances, which later proved to be highly significant for his life and his development, nothing was changed by his work. All that happened was that he became somewhat more aware of rising angers and that his symptoms disappeared.

Actually, any of the incidents that John happened to analyze could have yielded more insight than he gained from them. Thus in his analysis of the anger that emerged during the musical comedy there were numerous questions that he failed to touch on. What was the real nature of his relationship with his wife? Was the compatibility, of which he was proud, due only to compliance on his part? Was she domineering? Or was he merely hypersensitive to anything resembling coercion? Furthermore, why did he repress the anger? Was it necessary because of a compulsive need for affection? Was he apprehensive of a rebuke from his wife? Did he have to maintain an image of himself as a person who was never disturbed by "trifles"? Was he afraid of having to fight for his wishes? Finally, was he really only angry at the others for having overruled him, or was he primarily angry at himself for having given in because of sheer weakness?

The analysis of the anger following the staff meeting might also have opened up further problems. Why was he not more alert to his own interests when they were jeopardized? Again, was he afraid to fight for them? Or had the anger such dimensions—squashing the bedbugs —that it was safer to repress it altogether? Also, did he lay himself open to exploitation by being too compliant? Or did he experience something as exploitation which was actually merely a legitimate expectation of his co-operation? Furthermore, what about his wish to impress others—the memory of expecting admiration from his mother? Was his failure to impress his colleagues an essential element in his anger? And to what extent was he angry at himself for having been so unassertive? None of these problems was touched upon. John let the matter rest when he had discovered the effect of repressed anger at the others.

The second example is the experience that first set me to considering the possibility of self-analysis. Harry was a physician who came to me for analysis because of attacks of panic, which he tried to allay by taking morphine and cocaine; also he had spells of exhibitionistic impulses.

There was no doubt that he had a severe neurosis. After some months of treatment he went away on a vacation, and during this time he analyzed by himself an attack of anxiety.

The beginning of this piece of self-analysis was accidental, as it was in the case of John. The starting point was a severe attack of anxiety, apparently provoked by a real danger. Harry was climbing a mountain with his girl. It was strenuous climbing but not dangerous as long as they could see clearly. It became perilous, however, when a snowstorm arose and they were enveloped in a thick fog. Harry then became short of breath, his heart pounded, he became panicky and finally had to lie down to rest. He did not give the incident any thought but vaguely ascribed the attack to his exhaustion and to the actual danger. This is an example, by the way, of how easily we may be satisfied with wrong explanations *if we want to be,* for Harry was physically strong and anything but a coward in the face of an emergency.

The next day they went on a narrow path hewn into the steep, rocky wall of the mountain. The girl went ahead. The heartpounding started again when Harry caught himself at a thought or an impulse to push her down the cliffs. That naturally startled him, and, besides, he was devoted to her. He thought first of Dreiser's *American Tragedy,* in which the boy drowns his girl in order to get rid of her. Then he thought of the attack of the previous day and barely recaptured a similar impulse he had had then. It had been a fleeting one, and he had checked it as it arose. He remembered clearly, however, a mounting irritation against the girl before the attack, and a sudden wave of hot anger, which he had pushed aside.

This, then, was the meaning of the attack of anxiety: an impulse of violence born out of a conflict between a sudden hatred on the one hand, and, on the other, his genuine fondness for the girl. He felt relieved, and also proud for having analyzed the first attack and stopped the second.

Harry, in contrast to John, went a step farther, because he felt alarmed by his recognition of hatred and a murderous impulse toward the girl he loved. While continuing to walk he raised the question why he should want to kill her. Immediately a talk they had had the previous morning recurred to him. The girl had praised one of his colleagues for his clever dealing with people and for being a charming host at a party. That was all. And that could not have aroused this much hostility. Yet when thinking about it he felt a rising anger. Was he jealous? But there was no danger of losing her. This colleague, though, was taller than he, and non-Jewish (on both points he was hypersensitive), and he did have a clever tongue. While his thoughts were meandering along these lines he forgot his anger against the girl and focused his attention on comparing himself with the colleague. Then a scene occurred to him. He was probably four or five years old, and had tried to climb a tree but could not. His older brother had climbed it with ease and teased him from above. Another scene came back vividly when his mother praised this brother and he was left out. The older brother was always ahead of him. It must have been the same thing that infuriated him yesterday: he still could not stand to have any man praised in his presence. With this insight he lost his tenseness, could climb easily, and again felt tender toward the girl.

Compared with the first example, the second achieved in one way more and in another less. Despite the greater superficiality of John's self-analysis, he did take one step that Harry did not take. John did not rest satisfied when he had accounted for only one particular situation: he recognized the possibility that all his headaches might result from a repressed anger. Harry did not go beyond the analysis of the one situation. It did not occur to him to wonder whether his finding had a bearing on other attacks of anxiety. On the other hand, the insight that Harry arrived at was considerably deeper than John's. The recognition of the murderous impulse was a real emotional experience; he found at least an inkling of the reason for his hostility; and he recognized the fact that he was caught in a conflict.

In the second incident, too, one is astonished at the number of questions not touched upon. Granting that Harry became irritated at praise of another man, whence the intensity of the reaction? If that praise was the only source of his hostility why was it such a threat to him as to arouse violence? Was he in the grip of an excessively great and excessively vulnerable vanity? If so, what were the deficiencies in him that needed so much covering up? The rivalry with the brother was certainly a significant historical factor, but insufficient as an explanation. The other side of the conflict, the nature of his devotion to the girl, is entirely untouched. Did he need her primarily for her admiration? How much dependency was involved in his love? Were there other sources of hostility toward her?

Bill

A third example concerns the analysis of a kind of stage fright. Bill, a healthy, strong, intelligent, and successful lawyer, consulted me because of a fear of high places. He had a recurring nightmare in which he was pushed from a bridge or tower. He felt dizzy when he sat in the first row of a theater balcony and when he looked down from high windows. Also, he sometimes felt panicky before he had to appear in court or before he met important clients. He had worked up from a poor environment and was afraid of not being able to maintain the good position he had attained. The feeling often crept up on him that he was putting on a bluff and that it would be found out sooner or later. He could not account for this fear because he believed himself as intelligent as his colleagues; he was a good speaker and usually could convince others by his arguments.

Because he talked frankly about himself we managed to see in a few interviews the outlines of a conflict between, on the one side, ambition, assertiveness, a desire to put something over on others, and, on the other side, a need to maintain the appearance of a jolly straight fellow who did not want anything for himself. Neither side of the conflict was deeply repressed. He had merely failed to realize the strength and the contradictory nature of

163

these strivings. Once they were brought into sharp focus he recognized squarely that he actually did put up a bluff. He then spontaneously drew the connection himself between this inadvertent swindle and the dizziness. He saw that he craved to attain a high place in life but did not quite dare admit to himself how ambitious he really was. He was afraid that others would turn against him and push him down if they realized this ambition, and therefore he had to show a front of being a jolly good fellow to whom money and prestige did not mean much. Being nevertheless an essentially honest person, he was dimly aware of some bluff, which in turn had made him apprehensive of being "found out." This clarification sufficed to remove the dizziness, which was a translation of his fears into physical terms.

He then had to leave town. We had not touched upon his fear of public performances and of meeting certain clients. I advised him to observe the conditions under which his "stage fright" was increased or decreased.

Some time later I received this report. He had first thought that the fear appeared when the case he presented or the argument he used was debatable. But search in this direction did not lead very far, though he felt distinctly that he was not wholly wrong. Then he had a bad break which, however, proved to be a good break for his own efforts at understanding. He had prepared a difficult brief not too carefully, but was only moderately apprehensive about presenting it in court, for he knew that the judge was not too demanding. Then he learned that this judge had fallen ill, and that the one who would substitute was strict and unbending. He tried to console himself with the reminder that after all the second judge was far from vicious or tricky, but this did not diminish his rising anxiety. Then he thought of my advice and tried to let his mind run freely.

First an image appeared of himself as a small boy smeared from head to toe with chocolate cake. He was at first baffled by this picture, but then recalled that he was going to be punished but *got away with it* because he was so "cute" and his mother had to laugh about him. The theme of "getting by" persisted. Several memories emerged of times when he was not prepared at school, but got by. Then he thought of a teacher of history whom he hated. He could still feel the hatred. The class had to write a theme about the French Revolution. When returning the papers the teacher criticized his for being replete with high-sounding phrases but devoid of solid knowledge; he cited one of those phrases and the others roared with laughter. Bill had felt acutely humiliated. The English teacher had always admired his style but the history teacher seemed impervious to his charm. The phrase "impervious to his charm" took him by surprise, because he had meant "impervious to his style." He could not help feeling amused because the word "charm" expressed his true meaning. Sure enough, the judge was like the history teacher, impervious to his charm or his power of speech. That was it. He was accustomed to rely on his charm and his facility with words to "get by" instead of being thoroughly prepared. As a result he became panicky whenever he visualized a situation in which this tool would be ineffective. Since Bill was not deeply entangled in his neurotic trends he was able to draw the practical consequence of this insight: to sit down and work more carefully on the brief.

He even went a step farther. He realized to what extent he used his charm also in relationships with friends and women. Briefly, he felt that they should be under the spell of his charm and therefore overlook the fact that he did not give much of himself in any relationship. He linked this finding with our discussion by realizing that he had discovered another bluff, and he finished with the realization that he must "go straight."

Apparently he was able to do so to a considerable extent, because since that episode, which is now six years ago, his fears have practically disappeared. This result resembles the one attained by John when he overcame his headaches, but it must be evaluated differently. The headaches, as indicated before, were a peripheral symptom. They can be so designated by virtue of two facts: since they were infrequent and not severe they did not essentially disturb him; and they had not assumed any secondary function. John's real disturbances, as revealed in a subsequent analysis, lay in a different direction. Bill's fears, on the other hand, were the result of a crucial conflict. They did not handicap him but they interfered with significant activities in vital areas of his life. John's headaches disappeared without any concomitant change in his personality, the only change being a slightly greater awareness of anger. Bill's fears vanished because he recognized their source in certain contradictory trends in his personality and, more important, because he was able to change these trends.

Here again, as in John's case, the results seem greater than the efforts that produced them. But again on closer examination the disparity is not so great. It is true that with comparatively little work Bill managed not only to get rid of disturbances serious enough to jeopardize his career in the long run, but also to recognize a few important facts about himself. He saw that he had presented a somewhat deceptive front to himself and to others, that he was much more ambitious than he had admitted to himself, that he tended to attain his ambitious goals through his wits and his charm rather than through solid work. But in evaluating this success we must not forget that Bill, in contrast to John and Harry, was essentially a psychically healthy person with only mild neurotic trends. His ambition and his need to "get by" were not deeply repressed and did not have a rigid compulsive character. His personality was so organized that he could modify them considerably as soon as he recognized them. Dropping for a moment the effort to attain a scientific understanding of Bill's predicaments, one might regard him simply as a person who had tried to make life too easy for himself and who could do better when he realized that his way did not work.

Bill's insights were sufficient to remove certain gross fears. But even in this most successful short cut many questions are left open. What exactly is the meaning of the nightmare about being pushed down from a bridge? Was it necessary for Bill that he alone should be on top?

Did he want to push others down because he could not tolerate any competition? And was he therefore afraid others might do the same to him? Was his fear of high places only a fear of losing the position he had gained, or was it also a fear of falling down from a height of fictitious superiority—as it usually is in phobias of this kind? Furthermore, why did he not put in an amount of work commensurate with his faculties and his ambition? Did this laziness result only from the repression of his ambition, or did he feel that it would detract from his superiority if he made adequate efforts—that only mediocre people have to work? And why did he give so little of himself in his relations with others? Was he too engrossed in himself—or perhaps too contemptuous of others—to be able to experience much spontaneous emotion?

Whether it would be necessary, from the point of view of therapy, to pursue all such supplementary questions is another matter. In Bill's case it is possible that the little analysis done had farther reaching effects than the removal of conspicuous fears. It is possible that it set going something that might be called a beneficent circle. By recognizing his ambition and by putting in more work he would actually anchor his ambitions on a more realistic and more solid basis. Thereby he would feel more secure and less vulnerable and less in need of his bluff. By relinquishing the false front he would feel less constrained and less afraid of being found out. All of these factors might considerably deepen his relationships with others, and this improvement would also add to his feeling of security. Such a beneficent circle may have been set in motion even though the analysis was not complete. If the analysis had searched out all the untouched implications it would almost certainly have had this effect.

A last example leads us still farther away from a real neurosis. It concerns the analysis of a disturbance that was provoked mainly by the real difficulties in an actual situation. Tom was a medical assistant to a great clinician. He was deeply interested in his work and was favored by his chief. A genuine friendship had developed between them, and they often lunched together. Once after such a luncheon Tom had a mild stomach upset which he ascribed to the food, without giving it further attention. After the next luncheon with the chief he felt nauseous and faint, considerably worse than the first time. He had his stomach examined but there was no pathological finding whatever. Then the disturbance occurred a third time, now with a painful sensitivity to smells. Only after the third luncheon did it strike him that all these upsets had occurred when he was eating with the director.

As a matter of fact he had felt constrained with the director recently, sometimes not knowing what to talk about. And he knew the reason. His research work had led him in a direction which was opposite to the director's convictions. In recent weeks he had become more firmly convinced of his own findings. He had wanted to talk with the chief but somehow never got around to doing it. He was aware of procrastinating but the old man was rather rigid in scientific matters and did not easily tolerate dissension. Tom had shoved aside his concern by telling himself that a good talk would solve everything. If the stomach upset had to do with fears, he reasoned, then his fears must be much greater than he had admitted to himself.

He sensed that this was so and simultaneously had two proofs of it. One was that while having these thoughts he suddenly started to feel ill, just as he had felt after the luncheons. The other was that he realized just as suddenly what had started his reaction. During the luncheon in which the illness had first developed the director had made derogatory remarks about the ingratitude of Tom's predecessor. He had expressed his resentment against these young fellows, who learned much from him and then left and did not even bother to keep in touch with him on scientific matters. All that Tom felt consciously at that moment was sympathy for the chief. He had repressed his knowledge that actually what the director could not tolerate was that the predecessor had gone his own independent way.

Thus Tom became aware that he had closed his eyes to an existing danger, and he also recognized the extent of his fears. His work was creating a real danger to his good relationship with the director, and thereby a danger to his career. The old man might really turn against him. He felt somewhat panicky at this thought and wondered if it might be better for him to check his findings once more—or even forget about them. It was only a brief thought, but it showed him in a flash that this was

a conflict between his scientific honesty and the immediate exigencies of his career. By repressing his fears he
had pursued an ostrich policy, the purpose of which was
to avoid having to make a decision. With that insight he
felt free and relieved. He knew it was a hard decision but
did not doubt that it would be in favor of his conviction.

This story was told to me not as an example of self-
analysis but merely as an example of how great the temptation sometimes is not to be straight with oneself. Tom
was a friend of mine, an unusually well-balanced fellow.
Even though it is possible that he had certain hidden
neurotic tendencies, such as a need to deny any fears,
these did not make him a neurotic person. It might be
objected that the very fact of his unconsciously shirking
a decision was an expression of a deeper neurotic disturbance. But there is certainly no sharp borderline between
healthy and neurotic, and therefore it seems preferable
to leave it as a matter of emphasis and regard Tom for
all practical purposes as a healthy person. This episode
would then represent a situational neurosis, that is, a
neurotic upset caused primarily by the difficulties in a
particular situation and lasting only so long as the conflict is not consciously faced and solved.

Despite the fact that a critical estimate has been given
of the results attained in each of these examples, they
might, when regarded together, elicit an overoptimistic
impression about the potentialities of occasional self-
analysis, an impression that one can easily stumble over

an insight and pick up something precious. In order to convey a more adequate picture these four more or less successful attempts should be complemented by a review of twenty or more abortive efforts to grasp quickly the meaning of some psychic disturbance. It seems necessary to express explicitly such a cautious reserve because a person who feels helplessly caught in his neurotic entanglements tends to hope against hope for a miracle. It should be understood clearly that it is impossible to cure a severe neurosis, or any essential part of it, by occasional self-analysis. The reason is that the neurotic personality is not a piecemeal conglomeration—to use the expression of Gestalt psychologists—of disturbing factors, but has a structure in which each part is intricately interrelated to each other part. It is possible through occasional work at oneself to grasp an isolated connection here or there, to understand the factors immediately involved in an upheaval and to remove a peripheral symptom. But to bring about essential changes it is necessary to work through the whole structure, that is, it requires a more systematic analysis.

Thus occasional analysis, by its very nature, contributes but little to comprehensive self-recognition. As shown in the first three examples, the reason is that insights are not followed up. Actually each problem that is clarified automatically introduces a new one. If these leads that offer themselves are not picked up the insights necessarily remain isolated.

As a therapeutic method occasional self-analysis is entirely adequate for the situational neurosis. Also in

172

mild neuroses it can yield very satisfactory results. But in more intricate neuroses it is little more than a leap in the dark. At the very best it can do no more than release a tension here or there, or illuminate at random the meaning of one or another disturbance.

CHAPTER SEVEN

Systematic Self-Analysis: Preliminaries

Systematic self-analysis might be superficially distinguished from occasional analysis of oneself by the mere fact that it involves more frequent work: it, too, has its starting point in a particular difficulty which one wants to remove, but unlike occasional self-analysis it goes through the process over and over again, rather than resting content with an isolated solution. This description, however, while correct in a formalistic way, would miss the essential differences. One might recurrently analyze oneself and it would still remain occasional analysis if certain conditions were not fulfilled.

The greater frequency is one distinguishing factor in systematic self-analysis, but only one. More important is the attribute of continuity, the following up of problems; the lack of this in the examples of occasional work was emphasized in the previous chapter. This requires,

174

however, more than a mere conscientious picking up and elaboration of the leads that offer themselves. It is by no means from sheer superficiality or negligence that the persons in the examples cited were satisfied with the results attained. To proceed beyond insights that are within easy reach inevitably means to encounter "resistances," to expose oneself to all kinds of painful uncertainties and hurts and to take up the battle with these opposing forces. And this requires a different spirit from that which serves in occasional work. There the incentive is the pressure of some gross disturbance and the wish to resolve it. Here, though the work starts under a similar pressure, the ultimate driving force is the person's unrelenting will to come to grips with himself, a wish to grow and to leave nothing untouched that prevents growth. It is a spirit of ruthless honesty toward himself, and he can succeed in finding himself only to the extent that it prevails.

There is, of course, a difference between the will to be honest and the capacity to be so. Any number of times he will be unable to measure up to this ideal. There may be some consolation, however, in the fact that no analysis would be necessary if he were always transparent to himself. Furthermore, the capacity for honesty will gradually increase if he carries on with a measure of constancy. Each obstacle surmounted means gaining territory within himself and therefore makes it possible to approach the next with greater inner strength.

Feeling at a loss as to how to go about it, the person who is analyzing himself, however conscientious, may undertake the work with a kind of artificial zest. He may resolve, for instance, to analyze all his dreams from now on. Dreams, according to Freud, are the royal road to the unconscious. That remains true. But unfortunately it is a road that is easily lost if there is not full knowledge of all the territory around it. For anyone to try his skill at interpreting dreams without some understanding of the factors operating within himself at the time is a haphazard, hit-or-miss play. Interpretation may then degenerate into intellectual guesswork, even if the dream itself is seemingly transparent.

Even a simple dream may permit of various interpretations. For instance, if a husband dreams of his wife's death the dream may express a deep unconscious hostility. On the other hand, it may mean that he wants to separate from her and, since he feels incapable of taking this step, her death appears as the only possible solution; in this case the dream is not primarily an expression of hatred. Or, finally, it may be a death wish provoked by a merely transitory rage which had been repressed and found its expression in the dream. The problems opened up are different in the three interpretations. In the first one the question would be the reason for the hatred and for its repression. In the second it would be why the dreamer does not find a more adequate solution. In the third it would be the circumstances of the actual provocation.

Another example is a dream of Clare's during the period in which she tried to solve her dependence on her friend Peter. She dreamed that another man put his arm around her and said he loved her. He was attractive to her, and she felt happy. Peter was in the room, looking out of a window. The dream might suggest offhand that Clare was turning from Peter to another man, and thus be an expression of conflicting feelings. Or it might express a wish that Peter would be as demonstrative as this other man. Or it might represent a belief that turning to another attachment would solve the problem of her morbid dependency; in this case it would constitute an attempt to evade a real solution of the problem. Or it might express a wish to have a choice about remaining with Peter, a choice that she actually did not have because of her ties to him.

If some progress has been made toward understanding, then a dream may provide confirmation for an assumption; it may fill a gap in one's knowledge; or it may open up a new and unexpected lead. But if the picture is befogged by a resistance a dream is not likely to clarify matters. It may do so, but also it may be so intricately interwoven with unrecognized attitudes that it defies interpretation and merely adds to the confusion.

These warnings should certainly not deter anyone from attempts to analyze his dreams. John's dream about the bedbugs, for instance, was a definite help to him in understanding his feelings. The pitfall to be avoided is merely a one-sided concentration on dreams to the exclusion of other observations equally valuable. And a warning of an opposite character is equally important: we frequently have a compelling interest not to take a dream seriously, and by its very grotesqueness or exaggeration a dream may lend itself to such an ignoring of its message. Thus the first dream that will be presented in the next chapter, in reference to Clare's self-analysis, actually spoke a distinct enough language as to a serious turmoil in her relationship with her lover, yet she managed to take it lightly. The reason was that she had stringent reasons for not letting herself be moved by its implications. And this is not an exceptional situation.

Thus dreams are an important source of information, but only one among several. Since I shall not return to the interpretation of dreams, except in examples, I shall make a little detour here to mention two principles that are useful to keep in mind. One is that dreams do not give a photographic, static picture of feelings or opinions but are primarily an expression of tendencies. It is true that a dream may reveal to us more clearly than our waking life what our true feelings are: love, hatred, suspicion, or sadness otherwise repressed may be felt in dreams without constraint. But the more important characteristic of dreams is, as Freud expressed it, that they are governed by wishful thinking. This does not necessarily mean that they represent a conscious wish, or that they directly symbolize something we regard as desirable. The "wishful thinking" is likely to lie in the purport rather than in the explicit content. Dreams, in other words, give voice to our strivings, our needs, and often represent attempts at a solution of conflicts bothering us at the time. They are a play of emotional forces rather than a statement of facts. If two powerful contradictory strivings clash, an anxiety dream may result.

178

A basic diff. ∞ Fr & Jung : Fr: Conscious controls dreams
Jung: Dreams originate ⌐ unconscious

Thus if we dream of a person whom we consciously like or respect as a revolting or ridiculous creature we should look for a need that compels us to deflate that person rather than jumping to the conclusion that the dream reveals our hidden opinion of him. If a patient dreams of himself as a dilapidated house that is beyond repair, this may, to be sure, be an expression of his hopelessness, but the main question is what interest he has in presenting himself in this way. Is this defeatist attitude desirable for him as the lesser evil? Is it the expression of a vindictive reproach, at his own expense, revealing his feeling that something should have been done for him earlier but that now it is too late?

Dreams

The second principle to be mentioned here is that a dream is not understood until we can connect it with the actual provocation that stimulated it. It is not enough, for instance, to recognize in a dream derogatory tendencies or vindictive impulses in general. The question must always be raised as to the provocation to which this dream was a response. If this connection can be discovered we can learn a good deal as to the exact type of experience that represents to us a threat or an offense, and the unconscious reactions it elicits.

Another way of undertaking self-analysis is less artificial than a one-sided concentration on dreams but is, as it were, too presumptuous. A person's incentive to face himself squarely usually comes from a realization that his happiness or efficiency is being hampered by a certain outstanding disturbance, such as a recurring depression, chronic fatigue, chronic constipation of a functional character, general shyness, insomnia, a lifelong inhibition toward concentrating on work. And he is likely to attempt a frontal attack on the disturbance as such and set out on something of a blitzkrieg. In other words, he may try to get at the unconscious determinants of his predicament without knowing much of anything about his personality structure. The result, at best, will be that some sensible questions will occur to his mind. If his particular disturbance is an inhibition toward work, for example, he may ask himself whether he is too ambitious, whether he is really interested in the work he does, whether he regards the work as a duty and secretly rebels against it. He will soon get stuck and resolve that analysis does not help at all. But here the fault is his and cannot be put at the doorstep of psychoanalysis. A blitzkrieg is never a good method in psychological matters, but a blitzkrieg that is entirely unprepared is bad for any purpose. This would be one that has neglected any previous reconnoitering of the territory to be attacked. It is partly because ignorance in psychological matters is still so great and so widespread that anyone could even attempt such a dead-end short cut. Here is a human being with infinitely complex crosscurrents of strivings, fears, defenses, illusions; his incapacity to concentrate on work is one end result of the entirety of these factors. And he believes he can eradicate it by direct action, as simply as he switches off an electric light! To some extent this expectation is based on wishful thinking: he would like to remove quickly the disability that disturbs him; and he likes to think that apart from this outstanding disturbance everything is all right. He does not like to face the fact that an overt difficulty is merely an indication that something is basically wrong with his relation to himself and to others.

It is important for him, certainly, to remove his manifest disturbance, and certainly he should not pretend to be disinterested in it and artificially exclude it from his thinking. But he should keep it in the background of his mind as an area to be explored eventually. He must know himself very well before he can glimpse the nature of his concrete handicap. As he proceeds in the accumulation of this knowledge he will gradually assemble the elements involved in the disturbance, if he is alert to the implications of his findings.

In one way, however, the disturbances can be directly studied, for much can be learned by observing their vacillations. None of these chronic difficulties is equally strong all the time. The hold they have will tighten and lessen. At the beginning the person will be ignorant as to the conditions that account for these ups and downs. He may even be convinced that there are no underlying causes and believe that such vacillations are in the "nature" of the disturbance. As a rule this belief is a fallacy. If he observes carefully he will recognize a factor here and a factor there that contributes to making the condition better or worse. When he has once gained an inkling as to the nature of these contributing factors his capacity for further observation will be sharpened and thus he will gradually obtain a general picture of the relevant conditions.

181

The upshot of these considerations is the banal truth that if you want to analyze yourself you must not study only the highlights. You must take every opportunity to become familiar with this stranger or acquaintance that is yourself. This, by the way, is not a figurative way of speaking, for most people know very little about themselves, and only gradually learn to what extent they have lived in ignorance. If you want to know New York you do not merely look at it from the Empire State Building. You go to the lower East Side; you stroll through Central Park; you take a boat around Manhattan; you ride on a Fifth Avenue bus; and a great deal more. Opportunities to become familiar with yourself will offer themselves, and you will see them, provided you really want to know this queer fellow who lives your life. You will then be astonished to see that here you are irritated for no apparent reason, there you cannot make up your mind, here you were offensive without meaning to be, here you mysteriously lost your appetite, there you had an eating spell, here you could not bring yourself to answer a letter, there you were suddenly afraid of noises around you when alone, here you had a nightmare, there you felt hurt or humiliated, here you could not ask for a raise in salary or express a critical opinion. All these infinite observations represent that many entrances to the unfamiliar ground that is yourself. You start to wonder—which here, too, is the beginning of all wisdom—and by means of free association you try to understand the meaning of these emotional upsets.

Wonder

182

frequency
continuity
free association

Observations, and the associations and questions they arouse, are the raw material. But work on them takes time, as does every analysis. In a professional analysis a definite hour is set apart every day or every other day. This arrangement is expedient but it also has certain intrinsic values. Patients with mild neurotic trends can, without disadvantage, see the analyst merely when they are in trouble and want to discuss their difficulties. But if a patient in the clutches of a severe neurosis were advised to come only when he really wanted to, he would probably play hooky whenever he had strong subjective reasons for not going on, that is, whenever he developed a "resistance." This means that he would stay away when actually he needed the most help and when the most constructive work could be done. Another reason for regularity is the necessity to preserve some measure of continuity, which is the very essence of any systematic work.

Both reasons for regularity—the trickiness of resistances and the necessity to maintain continuity—apply, of course, to self-analysis as well. But here I doubt whether the observance of a regular hour would serve these purposes. The differences between professional analysis and self-analysis should not be minimized. It is much easier for anyone to keep an appointment with an analyst than with himself, because in the former instance he has a greater interest in keeping it: he does not want to be impolite; he does not want to expose himself to the reproach that he stayed away because of a "resistance"; he does not want to lose the value that the hour

183

might have for him; he does not want to pay for the time reserved for him without having utilized it. These pressures are lacking in self-analysis. Any number of things that apparently or actually permit of no delay would interfere with the time set apart for analysis.

A regular, predetermined time for self-analysis is unfeasible also because of inner reasons—and these quite apart from the subject of resistances. A person might feel like thinking about himself during a spare half hour before dinner but resent it as a nuisance at a prearranged time before he leaves for his office. Or he may not find any time during the day but have the most illuminating associations while taking a walk at night or while falling asleep. In this respect even the regular appointment with the analyst has certain drawbacks. The patient cannot see the analyst whenever he feels a particular urge or willingness to talk with him, but must appear at the analyst's office at the arranged time even if his zest to express himself is diminished. Because of external circumstances this disadvantage can scarcely be eliminated, but there is no good reason why it should be projected into self-analysis, where these circumstances are not present.

Still another objection to rigid regularity in self-analysis lies in the fact that this process should not become a "duty." The connotation of "have to" would rob it of its spontaneity, its most precious and most indispensable element. There is no great harm done if a person forces himself to his daily exercises when he does not feel like taking them, but in analysis listlessness

184

would make him lame and unproductive. Again, this danger may exist also in professional analysis, but there it can be overcome by the analyst's interest in the patient and by the very fact of the common work. In self-analysis a listlessness produced by overstressed regularity is not so easily dealt with, and it may well cause the whole undertaking to peter out.

Thus in analysis regularity of work is not an end in itself but is rather a means that serves the two purposes of preserving continuity and combating resistances. The patient's resistances are not removed because he always appears for his appointment at the analyst's office; his coming merely enables the analyst to help him understand the factors at play. Nor is consistent punctuality any guarantee that he will not jump from one problem to another and gain only disconnected insights; it is an assurance of continuity only for the work in general. In self-analysis, too, these requirements are essential, and I shall discuss in a later chapter how they can be fulfilled in a meaningful way. All that is important here is that they do not demand a rigid schedule of appointments with oneself. If a certain irregularity in work should make a person shirk a problem, it will catch up with him. And even at the expense of time it is wiser to let it slide until he himself feels that he had better go after it. Self-analysis should remain a good friend to fall back upon rather than a schoolmaster pushing us to make our daily good marks. Needless to say, this warning against compulsive regularity does not imply taking things easy. Just as a friendship must be cultivated if we want it to be a meaningful factor in our life, analytical work at ourselves can yield its benefits only if we take it seriously.

Finally, no matter how genuinely a person regards self-analysis as a help toward self-development rather than as a quick panacea, there is no use in his determining to pursue this work consistently from now until the day he dies. There will be periods in which he works intensely at a problem, such as the one described in the next chapter. But there will be other periods in which the analytical work at himself recedes into the background. He will still observe one or another striking reaction and try to understand it, thus continuing the process of self-recognition, but in distinctly diminished intensity. He may be absorbed in personal work or in group activities; he may be engaged in a battle with external hardships; he may be concentrated on establishing one or another relationship; he may simply feel less harassed by his psychic troubles. At these times the mere process of living is more important than analysis, and it contributes in its own way to his development.

The method in self-analysis is no different from that in work with an analyst, the technique being free associations. This procedure was fully discussed in Chapter Four, and certain aspects particularly relevant to self-analysis will be added in Chapter Nine. Whereas in working with an analyst the patient reports whatever comes into his mind, in working alone he begins by merely taking note of his associations. Whether he only notes them mentally or writes them down is a matter of individual preference. Some people can concentrate better when they write; others find their attention distracted by writing. In the extensive example cited in Chapter Eight some chains of associations were written, some were merely noticed and put down on paper afterward.

There are undoubtedly certain advantages in writing down one's associations. For one thing, almost everyone will find that his thoughts do not wander off on a tangent so easily if he makes it a rule to put down a short note, a catchword, of every association. At any rate he will notice the wandering more quickly. It may be, too, that the temptation to skip a thought or feeling as irrelevant is lessened when it is all down on paper. But the greatest advantage of writing is that it affords the possibility of going over the notes afterward. Frequently a person will miss the significance of a connection at first sight, but will notice it later when he lets his mind dwell on his notes. Findings or unanswered questions that are not well entrenched are often forgotten, and a return to them may revive them. Or he may see the old findings in a different light. Or he may discover that he has made no noticeable headway, but is essentially still at the same point where he was several months ago. These two latter reasons make it advisable to jot down findings, and the main paths leading up to them, even though they may have been arrived at without taking notes. The main difficulty in writing, the fact that thoughts are quicker than the pen, can be remedied by putting down only catchwords.

If most of the work is done in writing a comparison with diary-keeping is almost unavoidable, and an elaboration of this comparison may serve also to highlight certain characteristics of analytical work. The similarity with a diary suggests itself particularly if the latter is not a simple report of factual occurrences but is written with the further intention of truthfully recording one's emotional experiences and motivations. But there are significant differences. A diary, at its very best, is an honest recording of conscious feelings, thoughts, and motivations. The revealing character it may have concerns emotional experiences unknown to the outside world rather than experiences unknown to the writer himself. When Rousseau, in his *Confessions,* boasted of his honesty in exposing his masochistic experiences, he did not uncover any fact of which he himself was unaware; he merely reported something that is usually kept secret. Furthermore, in a diary, if there is any search for motivations, this does not reach beyond one or another loose surmise that carries little if any weight. Usually no attempt is made to penetrate beneath the conscious level. Culbertson, for instance, in *The Strange Lives of One Man,* frankly reported his irritation and moodiness toward his wife but gave no hint as to possible reasons. These remarks do not imply a criticism of diaries or autobiographies. They have their value, but they are intrinsically different from an exploration of self. No one can produce a narrative about himself and at the same time let his mind run in free associations.

There is still another difference which it is of practical

188

importance to mention: a diary often glances with one eye toward a future reader, whether that reader be the writer at a future time or a wider audience. Any such side glance at posterity, however, inevitably detracts from pristine honesty. Deliberately or inadvertently the writer is bound, then, to do some retouching. He will omit certain factors entirely, minimize his shortcomings or blame them on others, protect other people from exposure. The same will happen when he writes down his associations if he takes the least squint at an admiring audience or at the idea of creating a masterpiece of unique value. He will then commit all those sins that undermine the value of free associations. Whatever he sets down on paper should serve one purpose only, that of recognizing himself.

CHAPTER EIGHT

Systematic Self-Analysis of a

Morbid Dependency

No amount of description, regardless of how carefully it is presented, can convey an adequate impression of exactly what is involved in the process of reaching an understanding of oneself. Therefore instead of discussing this process in detail I shall present an extensive example of self-analysis. It deals with a woman's morbid dependency on a man, a problem which for many reasons is frequent in our civilization.

The situation described would be interesting enough if it were regarded merely as a common feminine problem. But its importance extends beyond the feminine sphere. An involuntary and in a deeper sense unwarranted dependency upon another person is a problem known to nearly everyone. Most of us deal with one or another aspect of it at one or another period of our lives, often recognizing its existence as little as Clare did when she started her analysis, and screening it instead behind such exquisite terms as "love" or "loyalty." This dependency is so frequent because it seems to be a convenient and promising solution for many troubles we all have. It puts grave obstacles, however, in the way of our becoming mature, strong, independent people; and its promise of happiness is mostly fictitious. Therefore a delving into some of its unconscious implications may be interesting and helpful, even apart from the question of self-analysis, to anyone who regards self-reliance and good relationships with others as desirable goals.

The woman who tackled this problem by herself is Clare, who has kindly allowed me to publish the story of her progress. Her background and analytical development have already been outlined, and thus I can dispense with many explanatory remarks that would otherwise be necessary.

But the main reason for selecting this report is neither the intrinsic interest of the problem it presents nor our knowledge of the person involved. Nor does this piece of analysis excel in brilliance or completeness. The reason is rather that with all its blunders and deficiencies the report shows clearly how a problem was gradually recognized and solved; even the blunders and deficiencies are sufficiently clear for discussion and sufficiently typical to make it possible to learn from them. It need hardly be emphasized that the process illustrated by this example is essentially the same in the analysis of any other neurotic trend.

The report could not well be published in its original form. On the one hand it has had to be elaborated, because it consists mostly of catchwords. On the other hand it has been abbreviated. For the sake of conciseness I have omitted those parts that are merely repetitious. Also, I have selected only that part of the report which is best rounded and which has a direct bearing on the problem of dependency, and have left out the earlier analytical endeavors to tackle the difficulties in the relationship, because they all ended in blind alleys. It would have been interesting to follow these futile attempts too, but it would not have added enough additional factors to justify the increased space required. Moreover, I have made only brief notes about the periods of resistance. In other words, the presentation on the whole deals only with the highlights of this particular analytical development.

Each aspect of the analysis, after a summary description, will be discussed. In these discussions several questions will be borne particularly in mind. What is the meaning of the findings? Which factors did Clare fail to see at the time? What are the reasons for her failure to see them?

After several months of not very productive efforts at self-analysis Clare awoke one Sunday morning with an intense irritation at an author who had failed to keep his promise to send an article for the magazine she edited. This was the second time he had left her in the lurch. It was intolerable that people should be so unreliable.

Soon after it struck her that her anger was out of proportion. The whole matter was scarcely of sufficient importance to wake her up at five in the morning. The mere recognition of a discrepancy between anger and alleged provocation made her see the real reason for the anger. The real reason also concerned unreliability, but in a matter more close to her heart. Her friend Peter, who had been out of town on business, had not returned for the week end as he had promised. To be exact, he had not given a definite promise, but he had said that he would probably be back by Saturday. He was never definite in anything, she told herself; he always aroused her hopes and then disappointed her. The fatigue she had felt the night before, which she had attributed to having worked too hard, must have been a reaction to her disappointment. She had canceled a dinner invitation because she had hoped for an evening with Peter, and then, when he did not show up, she had gone to a movie instead. She could never make any engagements because Peter hated to make definite dates in advance. The result was that she left as many evenings free as she possibly could, always harboring the disquieting thought, would he or wouldn't he be with her?

While thinking of this situation two memories occurred to her simultaneously. One was an incident that her friend Eileen had told her years before. Eileen, during a passionate but rather unhappy relationship with a man, had fallen seriously ill with pneumonia. When she recovered from the fever she found to her surprise that her feelings for the man had died. He tried to continue the relationship, but he no longer meant anything to her. Clare's other memory concerned a particular scene in a novel, a scene that had deeply impressed her when she was adolescent. The first husband of the novel's heroine returned from war, expecting to find his wife overjoyed at his return. Actually the marriage had been torn by conflicts. During the husband's absence the wife's feelings had changed. She did not look forward to his coming. He had become a stranger to her. All she felt was indignation that he could be so presumptuous as to expect love just because he chose to want her—as if she and her feelings did not count at all. Clare could not help realizing that these two associations pointed to a wish to be able to break away from Peter, a wish that she referred to the momentary anger. But, she argued, I would never do it because I love him too much. With that thought she fell asleep again.

Clare made a correct interpretation of her anger when she saw it as caused by Peter rather than by the author, and her interpretation of the two associations was also right. But despite this correctness the interpretations, as it were, lacked depth. There was no feeling whatever for the force of the resentment she harbored against Peter. Consequently she regarded the whole outburst as only a transient grievance, and thus discarded much too lightly the wish to tear loose from him. Retrospectively it is clear that at that time she was far too dependent on Peter to dare to recognize either the resentment or the wish for separation. But she had not the slightest aware-ness of any dependency. She ascribed the apparent ease with which she overcame the anger to her "love" for her friend. This is a good example of the fact that one will get no more out of associations than one can stand at the time, even though, as in this instance, they speak an almost unmistakable language.

Clare's basic resistance against the import of her associations explains why she did not raise certain questions that they suggested. It is significant, for example, that both of them, while connoting in a general way a wish to break off, indicated a very special form of breaking off: in both instances the woman's feelings faded out while the man still wanted her. As we shall see later on, this was the only ending of a painful relationship that Clare could visualize. To break away from Peter on her own initiative was unthinkable because of her dependency upon him. The idea that he could break away from her would have aroused sheer panic, though there are good reasons to infer that she felt deep down that he did not really want her while she hung on to him. Her anxiety on this score was so deep that it took her considerable time to realize the mere fact that she was afraid. It was so great that even when she discovered her fear of desertion she still closed her eyes to the rather obvious fact that Peter wanted a separation. In thinking of incidents in which the woman herself was in a position to reject the man Clare revealed not only a wish to be free but also a desire for revenge, both deeply buried and both referring to a bondage which was itself unrecognized.

Another question that she did not raise was why the

anger at Peter took a whole night to penetrate to awareness, and why, even then, it first concealed its true meaning by transferring itself to the author. The repression of her resentment is all the more striking as she was fully aware of her disappointment at Peter's staying away. Moreover, on such an occasion resentment would certainly have been a natural reaction, and it was not in her character never to allow herself to be angry at anyone; she often was angry at people, though it was characteristic of her to shift anger from its real source to trivial matters. But to raise this question, while apparently only a routine matter, would have meant to broach the subject of why the relationship with Peter was so precarious that any disturbance of it had to be shut out of awareness.

After Clare had thus managed to shake off the whole problem from her conscious mind she fell asleep again and had a dream. She was in a foreign city; the people spoke a language that she did not understand; she lost her way, this feeling of being lost emerging very distinctly; she had left all her money in the luggage deposited at the station. Then she was at a fair; there was something unreal about it but she recognized gambling stands and a freak show; she was riding on a merry-go-round which turned around more and more quickly so that she became afraid, but she could not jump off. Then she was drifting on waves, and she woke up with a mixed feeling of abandon and anxiety.

The first part of the dream reminded her of an experience she had had in adolescence. She had been in a strange city; had forgotten the name of her hotel and had felt lost, as in the dream. Also it came back to her that the night before, when returning home from the movie, she had felt similarly lost.

The gambling stands and the freak show she associated with her earlier thought about Peter making promises and not keeping them. Such places, too, make fantastic promises and there, too, one is usually cheated. In addition, she regarded the freak show as an expression of her anger at Peter: he was a freak.

What really startled her in the dream was the depth of the feeling of being lost. She immediately explained away her impressions, however, by telling herself that these expressions of anger and of feeling lost were but exaggerated reactions to her disappointment, and that dreams express feelings in a grotesque way anyhow.

It is true that the dream translated Clare's problems into grotesque terms, but it did not exaggerate the intensity of her feeling. And even if it had constituted a gross exaggeration it would not have been sufficient merely to dismiss it on that score. If there is an exaggeration it has to be examined. What is the tendency that prompts it? Is it in reality not an exaggeration but an adequate response to an emotional experience, the meaning and intensity of which are beyond awareness? Did the experience mean something quite different on the conscious and unconscious levels?

Judging from Clare's subsequent development, the latter question was the pertinent one in this instance.

Clare actually felt just as miserable, as lost, as resentful as the dream and the earlier associations indicated. But since she still clung to the idea of a close love relationship this realization was unacceptable to her. For the same reason she ignored that part of the dream about having left all her money in the luggage at the station. This was probably a condensed expression of a feeling that she had invested all she had in Peter, the station symbolizing Peter and also connoting something transitory and indifferent as opposed to the permanence and security of home. And Clare disregarded another striking emotional factor in the dream when she did not bother to account for its ending with anxiety. Nor did she make any attempts to understand the dream as a whole. She contented herself with superficial explanations of this and that element, and thus learned from it no more than she knew anyhow. If she had probed more deeply she might have seen the main theme of the dream as this: I feel helpless and lost; Peter is a great disappointment; my life is like a merry-go-round and I can't jump off; there is no solution but drifting; but drifting is dangerous.

We cannot discard emotional experiences, however, as easily as we can discard thoughts unconnected with our feelings. And it is quite possible that Clare's emotional experiences of anger and particularly of feeling lost, despite her blatant failure to understand them, lingered on in her mind and were instrumental in her pursuing the path of analysis she subsequently embarked upon.

198

The next piece of analysis still remains under the heading of resistance. While Clare was going over her associations the next day another memory occurred to her in connection with the "foreign city" of the dream. Once when she was in a foreign city she had lost her way to the station; since she did not know the language she could not ask directions and thus she missed her train. As she thought of this incident it occurred to her that she had behaved in a silly manner. She might have bought a dictionary, or she might have gone into any great hotel and asked the porter. But apparently she had been too timid and too helpless to ask. Then it suddenly struck her that this very timidity had played a part also in the disappointment with Peter. Instead of expressing her wish to have him back for the week end she had actually encouraged him to see a friend in the country so that he could have some rest.

An early memory emerged of her doll Emily, whom she loved most tenderly. Emily had only one flaw: she had only a cheap wig. Clare deeply wanted for her a wig of real hair, which could be combed and braided. She often stood before a toy shop and looked at dolls with real hair. One day she was with her mother in the toy shop, and the mother, who was generous in giving presents, asked her whether she would like to have a wig with real hair. But Clare declined. The wig was expensive and she knew that the mother was short of money. And she never got it, a memory which even now moved her almost to tears.

She was disappointed to realize that she had still not overcome her reluctance in expressing her wishes, despite the work on this problem during the course of her analytical treatment, but at the same time she felt tremendously relieved. This remaining timidity appeared to be the solution to her distress of the previous days. She merely had to be more frank with Peter and let him know her wishes.

Clare's interpretation illustrates how an only partially accurate analysis can miss the essential point and blur the issue involved. It also demonstrates that a feeling of relief does not in itself prove that the solution found is the real one. Here the relief resulted from the fact that by hitting upon a pseudo solution Clare succeeded, temporarily, in circumventing the crucial problem. If she had not been unconsciously determined to find an easy way out of her disturbance she would probably have paid more attention to the association.

The memory was not just one more example of her lack of assertiveness. It clearly indicated a compulsion to give first importance to her mother's needs in order to avoid becoming the object of even a vague resentment. The same tendency applied to the present situation. To be sure, she had been too timid in expressing her wish, but this inhibition arose less from timidity than from unconscious design. The friend, from all I gather, was an aloof person, hypersensitive to any demands upon him. At that time Clare was not fully aware of this fact, but she sensed it sufficiently to hold back any direct wishes concerning his time, just as she refrained from ever mentioning the possibility of marriage, though she often thought of it. If she had asked him to be back for the week end he would have complied, but with resentment. Clare could not have recognized this fact, however, without a dawning realization of the limitations within Peter, and this was still impossible for her. She preferred to see primarily her own share in the matter, and to see that part of it which she felt confident of overcoming. It should be remembered, too, that it was an old pattern of Clare's to preserve a difficult relationship by taking all blame on herself. This was essentially the way in which she had dealt with her mother.

The result of Clare's attributing the whole distress to her own timidity was that she lost—at least consciously —her resentment toward Peter, and looked forward to seeing him again. This happened the next evening. But a new disappointment was in store for her. Peter not only was late for the appointment but looked tired and did not express any spontaneous joy at seeing her. As a result she became self-conscious. He was quick to notice her freezing up and, as was apparently his habit, he took the offensive, asking her whether she had been angry at his not coming home for the week end. She answered with a weak denial but on further pressure admitted that she had resented it. She could not tell him of the pathetic effort she had made not to resent it. He scolded her for being childish and for considering only her own wishes. Clare was miserable.

In the morning paper a notice about a shipwreck

201

brought back to her that part of her dream in which she had drifted on waves. When she had time to think about this dream fragment four associations occurred to her. One was a fantasy of a shipwreck in which she was drifting on the water. She was in danger of drowning when a strong man put his arms around her and saved her. With him she had a feeling of belonging, and of never-ending protection. He would always hold her in his arms and never, never leave her. The second association concerned a novel which ended on a similar tone. A girl who had gone through disastrous experiences with a number of men finally met the man she could love and upon whose devotion she could rely.

Then she remembered a fragment of a dream that she had had at the time she became familiar with Bruce, the older writer who had encouraged her and implicitly promised to be her mentor. In that dream she and Bruce walked together, hand in hand. He was like a hero or a demigod, and she was overwhelmed by happiness. To be singled out by this man was like an indescribable grace and blessing. When recalling this dream Clare smiled, for she had blindly overrated Bruce's brilliance and only later had seen his narrow and rigid inhibitions.

This memory made her recall another fantasy, or rather a frequent daydream, which she had almost forgotten though it had played quite a role at college, before the time of her crush on Bruce. It circled around the figure of a great man, endowed with superior intelligence, wisdom, prominence, and wealth. And this great man made advances to her because beneath her inconspicuous exterior he had sensed her great potentialities. He knew that if given a good break she could be beautiful and achieve great things. He devoted all his time and energy to her development. He did not merely spoil her by giving her beautiful garments and an attractive home. She had to work hard under his guidance, not only at becoming a great writer but also at cultivating mind and body. Thus he made a beautiful swan out of an ugly duckling. It was a kind of Pygmalion fantasy, created from the point of view of the girl to be developed. Besides having to work at herself she had to be devoted to her master exclusively.

Clare's first interpretation of this series of associations was that they expressed a wish for an everlasting love. Her comment was that this is what every woman wants. She recognized, however, that this wish was enhanced at the present time because Peter did not give her a feeling of security and permanent love.

With these associations Clare actually touched rock bottom, but without becoming aware of it. The special characteristics of the "love" that she craved she saw only later on. Otherwise the most significant part of the interpretation is the statement that Peter did not give her what she wanted. It is made casually, as if she had known it all the time, but actually it was her first conscious realization of any deep dissatisfaction with the relationship.

It seems reasonable to speculate whether this apparently sudden realization was a result of the analytical work on the previous days. Of course the two recent disappointments had their share in it. But similar disappointments had occurred previously without Clare's arriving at such an insight. The fact that in the work done up to this point she had consciously missed all the essential factors would not invalidate such an assumption, because despite these failures two things did happen. In the first place, she had a strong emotional experience in the lost feeling that occurred in conjunction with the dream of the foreign city. In the second place, her associations, while at no point leading to a conscious clarification, nevertheless moved within an increasingly narrow circle around the crucial problem, and showed a degree of transparency that is usually present only when a person is close to an insight. We may wonder whether the mere fact of having such thoughts and feelings as emerged in Clare during this period helped to bring certain factors into sharper focus, even though they still remained beneath the conscious level. The premise underlying this speculation would be that not only the conscious facing of problems counts, but also every step taken forward toward this goal.

On the following days, however, in going over the last associations mentioned, Clare noticed more details. It struck her that in the first two associations of this series the man appeared as a savior. One man rescued her from drowning; the man in the novel offered the girl a refuge from abuse and brutality. Bruce and the great man of her daydream, while not saving her from any danger, also played a protective role. As she observed this repetitious motif of saving, shielding, sheltering, she realized that she craved not only "love" but also protection. She also saw that one of the values Peter had for her was his willingness and ability to give advice and to console her when she was in distress. A fact occurred to her in this context that she had known for quite a while—her defenselessness when under attack or pressure. We had discussed it together as one part of her having to take second place. She saw now that it produced, in turn, a need for somebody to protect her. Finally, she realized that her longing for love or marriage had always increased rather acutely whenever life became difficult.

In thus recognizing that a need for protection was an essential element in her love life Clare took a great step ahead. The range of demands that this apparently harmless need embraced, and the role it played, became clear only much later. It may be interesting to compare this first insight into a problem with the last one reported in regard to the same problem, the insight concerning her "private religion." The comparison reveals a happening frequent in psychoanalytical work. A problem is first seen in its barest outline. One does not recognize much beyond the fact that it exists. Later one returns to the same problem with a much deeper understanding of its meaning. The feeling would be unwarranted in such a case that the later finding is not new, that one has known it all along. One has not known it, at least not consciously, but the way for its emergence has been prepared.

Despite a certain superficiality this first insight struck the initial blow at Clare's dependency. But while she glimpsed her need for protection she did not yet realize its nature, and thus she could not draw the conclusion that this was one of the essential factors in her problem. She also ignored all the material in the daydream of the great man, material indicating that the man she loved was expected to fulfill many more functions than mere protection.

The next report to be discussed is dated six weeks later. The notes Clare made within those weeks do not contribute any new analytical material but they contain certain pertinent self-observations. These concern her inability to be alone. She had not been aware of this inhibition before, because she had arranged her life in such a way as to avoid any periods of solitude. She observed now that when she was by herself she became restless or fatigued. Things she was capable of enjoying otherwise lost their meaning when she tried to enjoy them alone. She could work much better in the office, when others were around, than at home, though the work was of the same kind.

During this time she neither tried to understand these observations nor made any effort to follow up her latest finding. In view of the incisive importance of that finding her failure to pursue it any further is certainly striking. If we consider it in connection with the reluctance she had previously shown to scrutinize her relationship with Peter, we are justified in assuming that with her latest discovery Clare came closer to realizing her dependency than she could stand at the time and therefore stopped her analytical endeavors.

206

The provocation to resume her work was a sudden sharp swing of mood that occurred one evening with Peter. He had given her an unexpected present, a pretty scarf, and she was overjoyed. But later she felt suddenly tired and became frigid. The depressed feeling occurred after she had embarked on the question of summer plans. She was enthusiastic about the plans, but Peter was listless. He explained his reaction by saying that he didn't like to make plans anyhow.

The next morning she remembered a dream fragment. She saw a large bird flying away, a bird of most glorious colors and most beautiful movements. It became smaller and smaller until it vanished. Then she awoke with anxiety and a sensation of falling. While she was still waking up a phrase occurred to her—"the bird has flown"—which she knew at once expressed a fear of losing Peter. Certain later associations confirmed this intuitive interpretation: someone had once called Peter a bird that never settled down; Peter was good looking and a good dancer; the beauty of the bird had something unreal; a memory of Bruce, whom she had endowed with qualities he did not possess; a wonder whether she glorified Peter, too; a song from Sunday school, in which Jesus is asked to take His children under His wing.

Thus the fear of losing Peter was expressed in two ways: by the bird flying away, and by the idea of a bird that had taken her under its wings and dropped her. The latter thought was suggested not only by the song but also by the sensation of falling that she had on awakening. In the symbol of Jesus taking His children under His wing the theme of the need for protection is resumed. In view of later developments it appears by no means accidental that the symbol is a religious one.

Clare did not delve into the suggestion that she glorified Peter. But the very fact that she saw this possibility is noteworthy. It may have paved the way for her daring to take a good look at him some time later.

The main theme of her interpretations, however—the fear of losing Peter—not only was recognized as an inevitable conclusion to be drawn from the dream but was deeply felt as true and important. That it was an emotional experience as well as an intellectual recognition of a crucial factor was evident in the fact that a number of reactions hitherto not understood became suddenly transparent. First she saw that on the previous night she had not merely been disappointed in Peter's reluctance to talk about a common vacation. His lack of zest had aroused a dread that he would desert her, and this dread had caused her fatigue and frigidity and had been the provocation for the dream. And many other comparable situations became similarly illuminated. All kinds of instances emerged in which she had felt hurt, disappointed, irritated, or in which, as on the preceding day, she had become tired or depressed apparently for no good reason. She realized that all these reactions sprang from the same source, regardless of what other factors might have been involved. If Peter was late, if he did not telephone, if he was preoccupied with other matters than herself, if he was withdrawn, if he was tense or irritated, if he was not sexually interested in her—always

208

the same dread of desertion was touched off. Furthermore, she understood that the explosions of irritation that sometimes occurred when she was with Peter resulted not from trivial dissensions or, as he usually accused her, from her desire to have her own way, but from this same dread. The anger was attached to such trivial matters as different opinions about a movie, irritation at having to wait for him, and the like, but actually it was produced by her fear of losing him. And, conversely, she was overjoyed when she received an unexpected present from him because to a large extent it meant a sudden relief from this fear.

Finally, she linked up the fear of desertion with the empty feeling that she had when she was alone, but without arriving at any conclusive understanding of the connection. Was the fear of desertion so great because she dreaded to be alone? Or did solitude, for her, implicitly mean desertion?

This part of the analysis strikingly illustrates the astonishing fact that a person can be entirely unaware of a fear that actually is all consuming. That Clare now recognized her fear, and saw the disturbances it created in her relationship with Peter, meant a definite step ahead. There are two connections between this insight and her preceding one concerning her need for protection. Both findings show to what extent the whole relationship was pervaded with fears. And, more specifically, the fear of desertion was in part a consequence of the need for protection: if Peter was expected to protect her from life and its dangers she could not afford to lose him.

Clare was still far from understanding the nature of the fear of desertion. She was still unaware that what she regarded as deep love was little, if anything, more than a neurotic dependency and therefore she could not possibly recognize that the fear was based on this dependency. The loose questions that occurred to her in this context, regarding her incapacity to be alone, were more pertinent than she realized, as will be seen later. But since this whole problem was hazy, because there were still too many unknown factors involved, she was not even capable of making accurate observations on this score.

Clare's analysis of her elation at receiving the scarf was accurate as far as it went. Undoubtedly one important element in her feeling overjoyed was that the act of friendliness allayed her fear for the time being. That she did not consider the other elements involved can scarcely be attributed to a resistance. She saw only the particular aspect that was related to the problem on which she was then working, her fear of desertion.

It was about a week later that Clare perceived the other elements involved in her elation at the gift. She was not usually given to crying in movies but on this particular evening tears came to her eyes when a girl who was in a wretched condition met with unexpected help and friendliness. She ridiculed herself for being sentimental but this did not stop the tears, and afterward she felt a need to account for her behavior. She first thought of the possibility that an unconscious unhappiness of her own might have expressed itself in crying about the movie. And, of course, she did find reasons for unhappiness. Yet her associations along this line of thought led nowhere. It was only the next morning that she suddenly saw the issue: the crying had occurred not when the girl in the movie was badly off but when her situation took an unexpected turn for the better. She realized then what she had overlooked the previous day —that she always cried at such occasions.

Her associations then fell in line. She remembered that in her childhood she always cried when she reached the point where the fairy godmother heaps unexpected presents on Cinderella. Then her joy at receiving the scarf came back to her. The next memory concerned an incident that had occurred during her marriage. Her husband usually gave her only the presents due at Christmas or on birthdays, but once an important business friend of his was in town and the two men went with her to a dressmaker to help her select a dress. She could not make up her mind which of two dresses to choose. The husband then made a generous gesture and suggested that she take both garments. Though she knew that this gesture was made not altogether for her sake, but also in order to impress the business friend, she nevertheless was inordinately happy about it and cherished these particular dresses more than others. Finally, two aspects of the daydream of the great man occurred to her. One was the scene in which, to her complete surprise, he singled her out for his favors. The other concerned all the presents he gave her, incidents that she had told herself in great detail: the trips he suggested, the hotels he chose, the gowns he brought home, the invitations to luxurious restaurants. She never had to ask for anything.

She felt quite taken aback, almost like a criminal who is confronted with overwhelming evidence. This was her "love"! She remembered a friend, a sworn bachelor, saying that woman's love is merely a screen for exploiting men. She also recalled her friend Susan who had greatly astonished her by saying that she thought the usual flood of talk about love was disgusting. Love, said Susan, was only an honest deal in which each partner did his share to create a good companionship. Clare had been shocked at what she regarded as cynicism: Susan was too hard boiled in denying the existence and the value of feelings. But she herself, she now realized, had naïvely mistaken for love something that largely consisted of expectations that tangible and intangible gifts would be presented to her on a silver platter. Her love was at bottom no more than a sponging on somebody else!

This was certainly an entirely unexpected insight, but despite the painful surprise at herself she soon felt greatly relieved. She felt, and rightly, that she had really uncovered her share in what made her love relationships difficult.

Clare was so overwhelmed by the discovery she had made that she quite forgot the incident from which she had started, the crying in the movie. But she returned to it the next day. The tears expressed an overwhelming bewilderment at the thought of a sudden fulfillment of most secret and most ardent wishes, a fulfillment of something one has waited for all one's life, something that one has never dared to believe would come true.

Within the next couple of weeks Clare followed up her insight in several directions. In glancing over her latest series of associations it struck her that in almost all the incidents the emphasis was on help or gifts that came unexpectedly. She felt that at least one clue for this lay in the last remark she had written about the daydream, which was that she never had to ask for anything. Here she came into territory that was familiar to her through the previous analytic work. Since she had formerly tended to repress her own wishes, and was still inhibited to some extent from expressing them, she needed somebody who wished for her, or who guessed her secret wishes and fulfilled them without her having to do anything about them herself.

Another tack she pursued concerned the reverse side of the receptive, sponging attitude. She realized that she herself gave very little. Thus she expected Peter to be always interested in her troubles or interests but did not actively participate in his. She expected him to be tender and affectionate but was not very demonstrative herself. She responded but left the initiative to him.

On another day she returned once more to her notes concerning the evening in which her mood had swung from elation to depression, and she saw the possibility of another factor that might have been involved in that fatigue. She wondered whether the latter might have resulted not only from the anxiety that had been aroused but also from a repressed anger for the frustration of her wishes. If that were so her wishes could not be quite so harmless as she had assumed, for they must then contain some admixture of an insistence that they be complied with. She left this an open question.

This piece of analysis had an immediately favorable influence upon the relationship with Peter. She became more active in sharing his interests and in considering his wishes, and ceased being merely receptive. Also, the sudden eruptions of irritation stopped entirely. It is hard to say whether her demands upon him relented, though it would be reasonable to assume that they did to a moderate degree.

This time Clare faced her finding so squarely that there is almost nothing to add. It is noteworthy, though, that the same material had presented itself six weeks before, when the daydream of the great man first emerged. At that time the need to hold on to the fiction of "love" was still so stringent that she could do no more than admit that her love was tinged with a need for protection. Even in that admission she could conceive of the need for protection only as a factor reinforcing her "love." Nevertheless, as mentioned before, that early insight constituted the first attack on her dependency. The discovery of the degree of fear in her love was the second step. A further step was the question she raised as to whether she overrated Peter, even though the question remained unanswered. And only after she had worked that far through the fog could she finally see that her love was by no means unadulterated. Only now could she stand the disillusionment of recognizing that she had mistaken for love her abundant expectations and demands. She did not yet take the last step of realizing the dependency that resulted from her expectations. Otherwise, however, this fragment of analysis is a good example of what it means to follow up an insight. Clare saw that her expectations of others were largely engendered by her own inhibitions toward wishing or doing anything for herself. She saw that her sponging attitude impaired her capacity to give anything in return. And she recognized her tendency to feel offended if her expectations were rejected or frustrated.

Actually Clare's expectations were mainly in reference to intangible things. Despite apparent evidence to the contrary, she was not essentially a greedy person. I would even say that the receiving of presents was only a symbol for less concrete but more important expectations. She demanded to be cared for in such a way that she should not have to make up her mind as to what is right or wrong, should not have to take the initiative, should not have to be responsible for herself, should not have to solve external difficulties.

Some weeks passed in which, on the whole, her relationship with Peter was smoother. They had finally planned a trip together. Through his long indecision he had spoiled for her most of the joy of anticipation, though when everything was settled she did look forward to the holiday. But a few days before they were to leave he told her that business was too precarious just then to allow him to leave town for any length of time. Clare was first enraged and then desperate, and Peter scolded her for being unreasonable. She tended to accept the reproach and tried to convince herself that he was right. When she calmed down she suggested that she go alone to a resort that was only a three-hour drive from the city; Peter could then join her whenever his time allowed. Peter did not openly refuse this arrangement, but after some hemming and hawing he said that he would have been very glad to agree to it if she were able to take things more reasonably, but since she reacted so violently to every disappointment, and since he was not master of his time, he foresaw only frictions forthcoming and felt it better for her to make her plans without him. This again threw her into despair. The evening ended with Peter consoling her and promising to go away with her for ten days at the end of the vacation. Clare felt reassured. Inwardly agreeing with Peter, she decided to take things more easily and to be content with what he could give her.

The next day, while trying to analyze her first reaction of rage, she had three associations. The first was a memory of being teased, when she was a child, for playing the martyr role. But this memory, which had often recurred to her, appeared now in a new light. She had never before examined whether the others were wrong in teasing her in this way. She had taken it merely as a fact. Now for the first time it dawned on her that they were not right, that she actually had been discriminated

against, that by teasing her they had added insult to injury.

Then another memory occurred to her from the time
when she was five or six. She used to play with her
brother and his playmates, and one day they told her
that in a certain meadow, near where they played, robbers lived in a hidden cave. She believed it completely
and always trembled when she went near that meadow.
Then one day they had ridiculed her for having fallen
for their story.

Finally she thought of her dream of the foreign city,
the part in which she had seen the freak show and the
gambling stands. And now she realized that these sym-
bols expressed more than a transient anger. She saw for
the first time that there was something phony, something
fraudulent in Peter. Not in the sense of any deliberate
swindle. But he could not help playing the role of one
who was always right, always superior, always generous
—and he had feet of clay. He was wrapped up in himself, and when he yielded to her wishes it was not because of love and generosity but because of his own weakness. Finally, in his dealing with her there was much
subtle cruelty.

Only now did she recognize that her reaction the
previous night was primarily due not to the disappointment but to the callousness with which he had disregarded her feelings. There had been no tenderness, no
regret, no sympathy when he broke to her the news of
having to stay in town. It was only toward the end of the

217

evening, when she cried bitterly, that he turned affectionate. In the meantime he had made her bear the brunt of the distress. He had impressed on her that everything was her fault. He had acted in exactly the same way as her mother and brother had acted in her childhood, first stepping on her feelings and then making her feel guilty. Incidentally, it is interesting to see here how the meaning of a fragment became clearer because she had picked up her courage to rebel, and how this elucidation of the past in turn helped her to become more straight in the present.

Clare then recalled any number of incidents in which Peter had made implicit or explicit promises and had not kept them. Moreover, she realized that this behavior showed itself also in more important and more intangible ways. She saw that Peter had created in her the illusion of a deep and everlasting love, and yet was anxious to keep himself apart. It was as if he had intoxicated himself and her with the idea of love. And she had fallen for it, as she had fallen for the story of the robbers.

Finally Clare recalled the associations she had had before that early dream: thoughts of her friend Eileen, whose love faded out during the illness, and the novel in which the heroine felt estranged from her husband. These thoughts too, she realized now, had a much more serious connotation than she had assumed. Something within her seriously wanted to break away from Peter. Though she was not happy about this insight she nevertheless felt relieved. She felt as if a spell had been broken.

In following up her insight Clare began to wonder

why it had taken her such a long time to obtain a clear picture of Peter. Once these traits in him were recognized they appeared so conspicuous to her that it was hard to overlook them. She saw then that she had a strong interest in not seeing them: nothing should prevent her from seeing in Peter the realization of the great man of her daydream. Also she saw for the first time the whole parade of figures whom she had hero-worshiped in a similar way. The parade started with her mother, whom she had idolized. Then Bruce had followed, a type in many ways similar to Peter. And the daydream man, and many others. The dream of the glorious bird now definitely crystallized as a symbol for her glorification of Peter. Always, because of her expectations, she had hitched her wagon to a star. And all the stars had proved to be candles.

The impression might prevail here that this discovery of Clare's was no discovery at all. Had she not realized long ago that Peter promised more than he kept? Yes, she had seen it some months before, but she had neither taken it seriously nor appreciated the whole extent of Peter's unreliability. At that time her thought had been predominantly an expression of her own anger at him; now it had crystallized to an opinion, a judgment. Moreover, she did not then see the admixture of sadism behind his façade of righteousness and generosity. She could not possibly have arrived at this clear vision as long as she blindly expected him to fulfill all her needs. Her realization that she had fantastic expectations, and her willingness to put the relationship on a give-and-

219

take basis, had made her so much stronger that she could now dare to face his weakness and thus shake the pillars on which the relationship rested.

A good characteristic of the course that Clare had adopted in her analysis was the fact that she first searched within herself for the sources of her troubles, and only after that work had proceeded looked into Peter's share in them. Originally her self-examination was an attempt to find an easy clue with which to solve the difficulties of the relationship, but it led her eventually to some important insights into herself. Anyone in analysis must learn to understand not only himself but also the others who are a part of his life, but it is safer to start with himself. As long as he is entangled in his conflicts the picture he will gain of the others will usually be a distorted one.

From the data about Peter that Clare assembled in the course of her entire analytical work I gather that her analysis of his personality was essentially correct. Nevertheless she still missed the one important point: that Peter, for whatever reasons of his own, was determined to break away from her. Of course, the assurances of love which he apparently never failed to give her must have befogged her judgment. On the other hand, this explanation is not quite sufficient, because it leaves open two questions: why her effort to reach a clear picture of him stopped where it did; and why she could visualize —though not put into effect—the desirability of her breaking away from Peter, but closed her eyes to the possibility of his breaking away from her.

As a result of this remaining tie Clare's wish to break off remained short lived. She was unhappy while she was away from him and as soon as he joined her she succumbed to his charm. Also, she still could not stand the prospect of being alone. Thus the relationship went on. She expected less of him and was more resigned. But her life still centered around him.

Three weeks later she woke up with the name Margaret Brooks on her lips. She did not know whether she had dreamed of her but she knew the meaning immediately. Margaret was a married friend whom she had not seen for years. She had been pitifully dependent on her husband despite the fact that he ruthlessly trampled on her dignity. He neglected her and made sarcastic remarks about her in front of others; he had mistresses and brought one of them into their home. Margaret had often complained to Clare in her spells of despair. But she always became reconciled and believed that hers would still turn out to be the best of husbands. Clare had been staggered at such a dependency and had felt contemptuous of Margaret's lack of pride. Nevertheless, her advice to Margaret dealt exclusively with means of keeping the husband or of winning him back. She had joined her friend in the hope that all would be fine in the end. Clare knew that the man was not worth it, but since Margaret loved him so much this seemed the best attitude to adopt. Now Clare thought how stupid she had been. She should have encouraged Margaret to leave him.

But it was not this former attitude toward her friend's situation that upset her now. What startled her was the similarity between herself and Margaret, which had struck her immediately upon awakening. She had never thought of herself as dependent. And with frightening clarity she realized that she was in the same boat. She, too, had lost her dignity in clinging to a man who did not really want her and whose value she doubted. She saw that she was bound to Peter with ties of overwhelming strength, that life without him was meaningless, beyond imagination. Social life, music, work, career, nature—nothing mattered without him. Her mood depended on him; thinking about him absorbed her time and energies. No matter how he behaved she still returned to him, as the cat is said to return to the house it lived in. During the next days she lived in a daze. The insight had no relieving effect. It merely made her feel the chains all the more painfully.

When she had recovered some degree of poise she worked through certain implications of her finding. She grasped more deeply the meaning of her fear of desertion: it was because her ties were essential to her that she had such a deep fear of their dissolution, and this fear was bound to persist as long as the dependency persisted. She saw that she had not only hero-worshiped her mother, Bruce, and her husband, but had been dependent upon them, just as she was upon Peter. She realized that she could never hope to achieve any decent self-esteem as long as injuries to her dignity meant nothing compared with the fear of losing Peter. Finally, she understood that this dependency of hers must be a threat and a burden to Peter, too; this latter insight made for a sharp drop in her hostility toward him.

Her recognition of the extent to which this dependency had spoiled her relations with people made her take a definite stand against it. This time she did not even resolve to cut the knot by separation. She knew, in the first place, that she could not do it, but also she felt that having seen the problem she could work it out within the relationship with Peter. She convinced herself that after all there were values in the relationship which should be preserved and cultivated. She felt quite capable of putting it on a sounder basis. Thus in the following month, in addition to her analytical work, she made real efforts to respect Peter's need for distance and to cope with her own affairs in a more independent fashion.

There is no doubt that in this piece of analysis Clare made an important advance. Indeed, she had discovered, quite by herself, a second neurotic trend—the first being her compulsive modesty—and a trend that she did not in the least suspect of existing. She recognized its compulsive character and the harm it did to her love life. She did not yet see, however, how it cramped her life in general, and she was far from recognizing its formidable strength. Thus she overrated the freedom she had gained. In this she succumbed to the common self-deception that to recognize a problem is to solve it. The solution of carrying on with Peter was actually only a compromise. She was willing to modify the trend to some extent but not yet willing to relinquish it. This was also the reason why, despite her clearer picture of Peter, she still underrated his limitations, which, as will be seen presently, were much greater and much more rigid than she believed. She also underrated his striving away from her. She saw it, but hoped that by a change in her attitude toward him she could win him back.

Some weeks later she heard that someone had spread slanderous remarks about her. It did not upset her consciously but led to a dream in which she saw a tower standing in an immense desert; the tower ended in a simple platform, without any railing around it, and a figure stood at the edge. She awoke with a mild anxiety.

The desert left her with an impression of something desolate and dangerous. And it reminded her of an anxiety dream in which she had walked on a bridge that was broken off in the middle. The figure on the tower meant to her merely a symbol of loneliness, which she actually felt, since Peter was away for some weeks. Then the phrase "two on an island" occurred to her. It brought back fantasies she occasionally had of being alone with a beloved man in a rustic cabin in the mountains or at the seashore. Thus at first the dream meant to her merely an expression of her longing for Peter and of her feeling alone without him. She also saw that this feeling had been increased by the report she had heard on the previous day, that is, she recognized that the slanderous remarks must have made her apprehensive and enhanced her need for protection.

224

In going over her associations she wondered why she had not paid any attention to the tower in the dream. An image occurred to her, which came to her mind occasionally, of herself standing on a column in the midst of a swampland; arms and tentacles arising from the swamp reached out for her as if they wanted to drag her down. Nothing more happened in this fantasy; there was only this picture. She had never paid much attention to it, and had seen only its most obvious connotation: a fear of being dragged down into something dirty and nasty. The slanderous remarks must have revived this fear. But she saw suddenly another aspect of the picture, that of putting herself above others. The dream of the tower had this aspect, too. The world was arid and desolate, but she towered above it. The dangers of the world could not reach her.

Thus she interpreted the dream as meaning that she had felt humiliated by the slanderous remarks and had taken refuge in a rather arrogant attitude; that the isolated height upon which she thus placed herself was frightening because she was much too insecure to stand it; that she had to have somebody to support her on this height and became panicky because there was nobody on whom she could lean. She recognized almost instantaneously the broader implication of this finding. What she had seen hitherto was that she needed somebody to support and protect her because she herself was defenseless and unassertive. Now she realized that she would occasionally swing to the other extreme, haughtiness, and

225

that in such situations she had to have a protector just as much as she did when she effaced herself. She was greatly relieved because she felt that she had glimpsed a new vista of ties fastening her to Peter, and thereby new possibilities of dissolving them.

In this interpretation Clare did in fact recognize another reason why she needed emotional support. There are good reasons why she had never seen this aspect of the problem. The whole area in her personality that consisted of arrogance, contempt for people, need to excel, need to triumph, was still so deeply repressed that as yet it had been illuminated only by flashes of insight. Even before she had started her analysis she had had occasional realizations of her need to despise people, of her great elation at any success, of the role ambition played in her daydreams, and it was a fleeting insight of this kind that she had now. But this whole problem was still so deeply buried that its manifestations could scarcely be understood. It was as if a shaft leading into the depths was suddenly lit up, and soon after obliterated by darkness. Thus another implication of this series of associations remained inaccessible. The picture of extreme solitude as presented in the tower in the desert referred not only to her feeling alone without Peter, but to her isolation in general. The subversive arrogance was one of the factors responsible for it, as well as resulting from it. And fastening herself to one person—"two on an island"—was a way of escaping from such isolation without having to straighten out her relations with people in general.

226

Clare believed that she could now cope with Peter in a better way, but soon afterward a double blow came which brought her problems to a climax. First she learned indirectly that he was having or had had an affair with another woman. She had barely received that shock when Peter wrote to her that it would be better for both of them if they separated. Clare's first reaction was to thank heaven that this had not occurred earlier. Now, she thought, she could stand it.

The first reaction was a mixture of truth and self-deception. The truth in it was that a few months before she probably could not have endured the stress without grave injury to herself; in the months to come she not only proved that she could stand it, but came closer to a solution of the whole problem. But this first matter-of-fact reaction apparently resulted also from the fact that she did not let the blow penetrate beneath a defensive armor. When it did penetrate, within the next few days, she was thrown into a turmoil of wild despair.

She was too deeply upset to analyze her reaction, which is understandable. When a house is on fire one does not reflect on causes and effects but tries to get out. Clare recorded two weeks later that for a few days the idea of suicide kept recurring to her, though it never assumed the character of a serious intention. She quickly became aware of the fact that she was merely playing around with the idea, and she then faced herself squarely with the question whether she wanted to die or to live. She definitely did want to live. But if she did not want to live as a wilting flower she not only had to rid herself of her longing for Peter, and the feeling that her life was smashed to pieces by losing him, but also to overcome radically her whole problem of compulsive dependency.

As soon as the issue was thus clear in her mind a struggle set in of unexpected intensity. It was only now that she felt the unmitigated power of her need to merge with another person. There was no more fooling around with the persuasion that it was "love": she realized it was like a drug addiction. She saw with perfect clarity that she had only the two alternatives of succumbing to the dependency, and finding another "partner," or overcoming it altogether. But could she overcome it? And was life worth living without it? She tried frantically and pathetically to persuade herself that after all life offered her many good things. Did she not have a nice home? Could she not find satisfaction in work? Did she not have friends? Could she not enjoy music and nature? It did not work. It all seemed as unappealing and irrelevant as the intermission in a concert. An intermission was all right—one marked time as pleasantly as possible until the music started again—but no one would want to go merely to the intermission. It struck her only fleetingly that this reasoning was thoroughly inapplicable. The feeling prevailed that any real change was beyond her strength.

Finally a thought occurred to her which despite its profound simplicity brought a turn for the better. It was the old wisdom that often an "I can't" is an "I won't." Perhaps she simply did not want to put her life on a different basis? Perhaps she actively refused to turn to anything else in life, like a child who refuses to eat anything if he does not get apple pie? Since she had recognized her dependency she had merely seen that her being caught hand and foot in the one relationship had so sapped her energies that nothing was left for anybody else. Now she realized that it was more than a mere drainage of interests. She herself rejected and devaluated everything she did on her own, or with anybody but the "beloved." Thus it dawned on her, for the first time, how deeply she was caught in a circle: her devaluation of everything outside the one relationship necessarily made the partner in that relationship all important; and this unique importance in turn alienated her more widely from herself and others. This dawning insight, which later proved to be right, startled her and encouraged her. If forces were operating within herself which prevented her from becoming free from captivity, then perhaps she could do something about her bondage.

This period of inner turmoil thus ended with Clare's obtaining a new lease on life and a renewed incentive to work at the problem. But here a number of questions arise. What about the value of the foregoing analytical work if the loss of Peter could still upset her as deeply as it did? Two considerations have a bearing on this question.

One is the insufficiency of the previous work. Clare had recognized the fact that she was compulsively dependent, and had seen certain implications of this condition. But she was far from reaching a real grasp on the problem. If one doubts the value of the work accomplished one makes much the same mistake that Clare herself made during the whole period before the climax, underrating the import of the particular neurotic trend and therefore expecting too quick and too easy results.

The other consideration is that on the whole the final upheaval was itself of a constructive nature. It represented the culminating point of a line of development that runs from a complete ignorance of the problem involved, and the most vigorous unconscious attempts to deny its existence, to a final full realization of its severity. The climax brought it home to her that her dependency was like a cancerous growth which cannot be kept within safe boundaries (compromises) but must be eradicated lest one's life be gravely jeopardized. Under the pressure of the acute distress Clare succeeded, too, in bringing into sharp conscious focus a conflict which had hitherto been unconscious. She had been entirely unaware of being torn between wanting to relinquish her dependency on another person and wanting to continue it. This conflict had been camouflaged by her compromise solutions with Peter. Now she had faced it, and was able to take a clear stand as to the direction in which she wanted to go. In this regard the phase she was now going through illustrates a fact mentioned in a previous chapter, that at certain periods in analysis it is necessary to take a stand, to make a decision. And it must be reckoned as an achievement if through the analytical work a conflict has sufficiently crystallized for the patient to be able to do this. In Clare's case the issue, of course, was whether or not she would immediately try to replace the lost pillar with a new one.

Naturally it is upsetting to face a problem in that uncompromising way. And here a second question comes in. Did Clare's experience produce a greater danger of suicide than it would have without analysis? For a consideration of this question it is relevant that she had indulged in suicidal notions at previous times. She had never, however, been able to terminate them so decisively as she did this time. Formerly they had simply faded out of the picture because something "nice" happened. Now she refuted them actively, consciously, and with a constructive spirit. Also, as mentioned above, her first reaction of gratefulness that Peter had not withdrawn earlier was in part a genuine feeling that she was now more capable of coping with his desertion. It seems safe to assume, therefore, that the suicidal tendencies would have been stronger and more persistent without the analytical work that was done.

A final question is whether Clare would have recognized the full severity of her entanglement without the external pressure exerted by Peter's breaking away from her. It might be thought that Clare, having passed through the development that occurred before the separation, could not possibly have stopped permanently at an essentially untenable compromise solution, but would have gone on sooner or later. On the other hand, the forces opposing her final liberation had great strength, and she might still have gone to considerable lengths to

231

make further compromises. This would be an idle speculation not worth mentioning if it did not touch upon an
attitude toward analysis not infrequent among analysts
as well as patients. This attitude is an assumption that
analysis alone is able to solve everything. But when treatment is endowed with such omnipotence it is forgotten
that life itself is the best therapist. What analysis can do
is to make one able to accept the help that life offers,
and to profit from it. And it had done exactly this job
in Clare's case. It is probable that without the analytical
work that she accomplished she would have reached out
for a new partner as soon as possible, and thus perpetuated the same pattern of experience. The important
point is not whether she could have freed herself without outside help but whether, when that help came, she
was able to turn it into a constructive experience. And
this she did.

As to the content of Clare's findings in this period,
the most important one was the discovery of an active
defiance against living her own life, feeling her own feelings, thinking her own thoughts, having her own interests and plans, in short against being herself and finding the center of gravity within herself. In contrast to
her other findings, this one was merely an emotional insight. She did not arrive at it by way of free association,
and there were no facts to substantiate it. Nor did she
have any inkling of the nature of the opposing forces;
she merely felt their existence. Retrospectively we can
understand why she could hardly have gone any further
at that point. Her situation was comparable to that of a

232

person who is driven from his homeland and confronted with the task of putting his whole life on a new basis. Clare had to make a fundamental change in her attitude toward herself and in her relations with others. Naturally she was bewildered by the complexity of this prospect. But the main reason for the blockage was that, despite her determination to solve the problem of dependency, there were still powerful unconscious forces preventing a final solution. She was, as it were, hanging in mid-air between two ways of dealing with life, not ready to leave the old and not ready to reach out for the new.

In consequence the following weeks were characterized by ups and downs in quick succession. She wavered between times in which the experience with Peter and all that it entailed appeared as part of a far-distant past, and others in which she desperately longed to win him back. Solitude, then, was felt as an unfathomable cruelty perpetrated on her.

In one of these latter days, going home alone from a concert, she found herself thinking that everyone was better off than she. But, she argued, other people are alone, too. Yes, but they like it. But people who have accidents are worse off. Yes, but they are taken care of in hospitals. And what about the unemployed? Yes, they are badly off, but they are married. At this point she suddenly saw the grotesqueness of her way of arguing. After all, not all the unemployed were happily married; and, even if they were, marriage was not a solution for everything. She recognized that a tendency must be at work which made her talk herself into an exaggerated misery. The cloud of unhappiness was dispelled and she felt relieved.

When she began to analyze this incident the melody of a song from Sunday school occurred to her, without her being able to recall the text. Then an emergency operation she had had to have for appendicitis. Then the "neediest cases" published at Christmas. Then a picture of a huge crevice in a glacier. Then a movie in which she had seen that glacier; somebody had fallen into the crevice and was pulled out at the last moment. Then a memory from the time when she was about eight years old. She was crying in bed and felt it was unthinkable that her mother would not come and console her. She did not know whether a quarrel with her mother had gone before. All she recalled was the unshakable conviction that her mother would be moved by her distress. The mother actually did not come, and she fell asleep.

Presently she recalled the text of the melody from Sunday school. It declared that no matter how great our sorrow, God will help us if we pray to Him. She suddenly saw the clue to her other associations and to the exaggerated misery that had preceded them: she had an expectation that great distress would bring about help. And for the sake of this unconscious belief she made herself more miserable than she was. It was shockingly silly, yet she had done it, and had done it frequently. In the crying spells, which had incidentally vanished com-

234

pletely, she had done exactly that. And she remembered any number of occasions when she had felt herself the most abused of all mortals, only to realize some time later that she had made matters much worse than they actually were. When she had been in the spell of such unhappiness, however, the reasons for it looked, and even felt, real. At such times she had often telephoned Peter, and he was usually sympathetic and helpful. In this regard she could almost count on him; here he had failed her less than anybody else. Perhaps this was a more important tie than she had realized? But sometimes Peter had not taken her unhappiness at its face value and had teased her about it, as her mother and brother had teased her in childhood. Then she had felt deeply offended and was furious with him.

Yes, there was a clear pattern that repeated itself— exaggerated misery and at the same time an expectation of help, consolation, encouragement, from her mother, from God, from Bruce, from her husband, from Peter. Her playing the martyr role, apart from everything else, must have been also an unconscious plea for help.

Clare was thus on the verge of recognizing another important clue to her dependency. But a day or so later she started to argue against her finding on two grounds. One was that it was nothing unusual, after all, to expect friendliness from a friend in bad times. What else was the value of friendship! Everybody is good to you if you are gay and contented. But with your sorrows you can go only to a friend. The other ground for disproving her finding was a doubt that it was applicable to the misery of the evening on which it had emerged. She had exaggerated her unhappiness, to be sure, but no one had been there to impress, no Peter could be telephoned. She could not possibly be so irrational as to believe that help would come merely because she made herself feel the most miserable of human beings. Yet sometimes when she felt bad something good did happen. Somebody would call her up or invite her out. She would receive a letter, her work would be praised, music on the radio would cheer her up.

She did not immediately notice that she argued for two contradictory points: that it was irrational to expect help as a direct result of feeling distressed; and that it was rational. But she saw the contradiction when she reread her notes some days later, and then she drew the only sensible conclusion, which was that she must have attempted to argue herself out of something.

She tried first to explain her equivocal reasoning on the basis that she felt a general distaste at finding in herself anything so irrational as an expectation of magic help—but this did not satisfy her. This, by the way, was an important clue. If we find an irrational area in an otherwise rational person we can be sure that it hides something important. The fight that is often put up against the quality of irrationality is usually in reality a fight against having its background uncovered. This held true here, too. But even without such reasoning Clare realized soon after that the real stumbling block was not the irrationality per se, but her resistance against facing her finding. She recognized that a belief that she

236

could command help through misery actually had a strong hold upon her.

Within the next months she saw with a gradually increasing measure of lucidity and in great detail what this belief did to her. She saw that she unconsciously tended to make a major catastrophe out of every difficulty that arose in her life, collapsing into a state of complete helplessness, with the result that despite a certain front of bravery and independence her prevailing feeling toward life was one of helplessness in the face of overwhelming odds. She recognized that this firm belief in forthcoming help had amounted to a kind of private religion, and that not unlike a true religion it had been a powerful source of reassurance.

Clare also acquired a deepened insight as to the extent to which her reliance on someone else had taken the place of reliance on herself. If she always had someone who taught her, stimulated her, advised her, helped her, defended her, gave her affirmation of her value, there was no reason why she should make any effort to overcome the anxiety involved in taking her life into her own hands. Thus the dependent relationship had so completely fulfilled its function of allowing her to cope with life without having to rely on herself that it had robbed her of any real incentive to abandon the small-girlish attitude entailed in her compulsive modesty. In fact, the dependency had not only perpetuated her weakness by stifling her incentive to become more self-reliant but it had actually created an interest in remaining helpless. If she remained humble and self-effacing all hap-

237

piness, all triumph would be hers. Any attempt at greater self-reliance and greater self-assertion was bound to jeopardize these expectations of a heaven on earth. This finding, incidentally, sheds light on the panic she felt at her first steps toward asserting her opinions and wishes. The compulsive modesty had not only given her the sheltering cloak of inconspicuousness, but it had also been the indispensable basis for her expectations of "love."

She realized it was merely a logical consequence, then, that the partner to whom she ascribed the godlike role of magic helper—to use a pertinent term of Erich Fromm's—became all important, and that to be wanted and loved by him became the only thing that mattered. Peter, through his peculiar qualities—apparently he was the savior type—was particularly fitted to play this role. His importance to her was not merely the importance of a friend who can be called upon in any time of real distress. His importance lay in the fact that he was an instrument whose services she could demand by making her need for them sufficiently great.

As a result of these insights she felt much more free than ever before. The longing for Peter, which at times had been excruciatingly strong, started to recede. More important, the insight brought about a real change in her objectives in life. She had always consciously wanted to be independent, but in her actual life had given this wish mere lip service and had reached out for help in any difficulty that arose. Now to become able to cope with her own life became an active, alive goal.

The only critical comment to be made on this piece of analysis is that it neglected the specific issue involved at that particular time: Clare's incapacity to be alone. Since I do not want to miss any opportunity to show how to go after a problem I shall mention two slightly different ways in which this one might have been approached.

Clare could have started from the consideration that her spells of misery had already decreased markedly within the last year. They had decreased to such an extent that she herself dealt more actively with external and internal difficulties. This consideration would have led to the question of why she had to resort to the old technique at just this point. Granted that she was unhappy alone, why did solitude present such an intolerable distress as to call for an instantaneous remedy? And if being alone was thus distressing why could she not do something actively about it herself?

Clare could also have started from an observation of her actual behavior. She felt miserable when alone, but she made hardly any effort to mix with friends or to make new contacts; instead she withdrew into a shell and expected magic help. Despite her otherwise astute self-observation Clare overlooked completely how odd her actual behavior was on this score. Such a blatant blind spot usually points to a repressed factor of great potency.

But, as I said in the previous chapter, if we miss a problem it catches up with us. This problem caught up with Clare some weeks later. She then arrived at a solution by a somewhat different route from either of those I have suggested—an illustration of the fact that also in psychological matters there are several roads to Rome. Since there is no written report on this part of her analysis I shall merely indicate the steps that led up to the new insight.

The first was a recognition that she could see herself only in the reflected light of others. The way in which she sensed that others evaluated her entirely determined the way she evaluated herself. Clare did not recall how she arrived at that insight. She remembered only that it suddenly struck her so forcibly that she almost fainted.

The meaning of this insight is so well elucidated by a nursery rhyme that I cannot resist the temptation to quote it:

> There was an old woman
> As I have heard tell
> She went to market
> Her eggs for to sell.
> She went to market
> All on a market-day
> And fell asleep
> On the king's highway.
>
> By came a peddler
> His name was Stout
> He cut off her petticoat
> All round about.
> He cut off her petticoat
> Up to her knees

Which made the old woman
Shiver and freeze.

When the old woman
First did awake
She began to shiver
And then to shake.
She began to wonder
And then to cry,
"Mercy on me
This is not I.

"But if it be I
As I hope it be
I have a little dog at home
And he will know me.
If it be I
He'll wag his little tail
If it be not I
He'll bark and he'll wail."

Home went the little woman
All in the dark
Up jumped the little dog
And began to bark.
He began to bark
And she began to cry,
"Mercy on me
This is not I."

241

The second step, which followed two weeks later, concerned more directly her revolt against being alone. Her attitude about this problem had changed since her analysis of the "private religion." She still felt the sting of being alone as keenly as before, but instead of succumbing to a helpless misery she had taken active steps to avoid solitude. She sought the company of others and enjoyed it. But for about a week she was entirely obsessed by the idea that she must have a close friend. She felt like asking all the people she met, hairdresser, dressmaker, secretary, married friends, whether they did not know a man who would be suitable for her. Everybody who was married or who had a close friend she regarded with the most intense envy. These thoughts assumed such proportions that it finally struck her that all of this was not only pathetic but definitely compulsive.

Only now was she able to see that her incapacity to be alone had greatly increased during the relationship with Peter, and had reached a climax after the separation. She realized, too, that she could endure solitude if it was of her own choosing. It turned painful only if it was not voluntary; then she felt disgraced, unwanted, excluded, ostracized. Thus she realized that the problem was not a general incapacity to be alone, but a hypersensitivity to being rejected.

Linking this finding with her recognition that her self-evaluation was entirely determined by the evaluation of others, she understood that for her the mere absence of attention meant that she was thrown to the dogs. That this sensitivity to rejection had nothing whatever to do with whether she liked those who rejected her, but concerned solely her self-esteem, was brought home to her by a memory from college. There had been in college a group of snobbish girls who had formed a close clique from which they had excluded her. She had no respect or liking for these girls but there had been moments when she would have given everything to belong to them. In this context Clare also thought of the close community between her mother and brother, from which she had been excluded. Incidents emerged in which she had been made to feel that in their eyes she was only a nuisance.

She realized that the reaction she discovered now had actually started at the time when she had stopped rebelling against discriminatory treatment. Up to that point she had had a native assurance that she was as good as the others, and had spontaneously reacted against being treated like an inferior being. But in the long run the isolation inevitably engendered by her opposition was more than she could stand, as was shown in the second chapter. In order to be accepted by the others she had knuckled under, had accepted the implicit verdict that she was inferior, and had begun to admire the others as superior beings. Under the stress of overwhelming odds she had dealt the first blow to her human dignity.

She understood then that Peter's breaking away from her had not only put her on her own, at a time when she was still rather dependent, but in addition had left her with a feeling of utter worthlessness. The combination of the two factors was responsible for the deep shock effect of the break. It was the feeling of worthlessness

243

that had rendered it intolerable to be alone. This feeling had first called for a magic remedy and had then produced an obsessive desire for a close friend as a means of rehabilitation. This insight brought about an immediate change. The wish for a man friend lost its compulsive character and she could be alone without feeling uneasy; she could even enjoy it at times.

She saw, too, how her reaction to being rejected had operated during the unfortunate relationship with Peter. Retrospectively she recognized that Peter had started to reject her in subtle ways soon after the first excitement of a love affair was gone. Through his withdrawing techniques and the irritability he showed in her presence he had indicated in ever-increasing degree that he did not want her. To be sure, this retreat had been disguised by the assurances of love he had given her simultaneously, but it could be effectively disguised only because she had blinded herself to the evidence that he wanted to get away from her. Instead of recognizing what she must have known she had made ever-increasing efforts to keep him, efforts that were determined by a desperate need to restore her own self-regard. Now it was clear to her that these very efforts to escape humiliation had injured her dignity more than anything else.

These efforts had been particularly pernicious since they involved not only an uncritical bending to Peter's wishes but also an unconscious inflation of her feeling for him. She realized that the more her actual feeling for him diminished the more she had worked it up to a pitch of false emotion, thus ensnaring herself still more deeply in her bondage. Her insights into the needs that constituted this "love" had lessened the tendency toward an inflation of feelings, but it was only now that her feelings dropped sharply to their actual level; in all simplicity she discovered that she felt very little for him. This recognition gave her a feeling of serenity that she had not had for a long time. Instead of wavering between longing for Peter and wanting to take revenge she took a calm stand toward him. She still appreciated his good qualities but she knew that it would be impossible for her ever to be closely associated with him again.

With this last finding to be reported here Clare tackled the dependency from a new angle. The work done up to this point can be summarized as a gradual recognition that she was dependent because of her huge expectations of the partner. She had realized step by step the nature of these expectations, this work culminating in the analysis of the "private religion." Now she saw in addition how the loss of spontaneous self-confidence had contributed to the dependency in a more direct way. The crucial finding in this regard was the recognition that her picture of herself was entirely determined by the evaluation of others. It is in accord with the significance of this insight that it struck her so deeply that she almost fainted; the emotional recognition of this tendency constituted an experience so deep that for a short moment it almost overwhelmed her. The insight did not in itself solve the problem but it was the basis for recognizing the inflation of her feelings and the far-reaching significance that "rejection" had for her.

245

CHAPTER NINE

Spirit and Rules

of Systematic Self-Analysis

Since we have already discussed psychoanalytic work from several points of view, and have seen from an extensive example the general procedure in psychoanalyzing oneself, it is scarcely necessary—and would indeed be repetitious—to discuss systematically the technique of self-analysis. The following remarks will therefore merely emphasize certain considerations, many of them already mentioned in other contexts, which deserve special attention when proceeding on one's own.

As we have seen, the process of free association, of frank and unreserved self-expression, is the starting point and continuous basis of all analytic work—self-analysis as well as professional analysis—but it is not at all easy of achievement. It might be thought that this process is

247

easier when working alone, for then there is no one who may appear to misunderstand, criticize, intrude, or retaliate; besides, it is not so humiliating to express to oneself those things of which one may be ashamed. To some extent this is true, although it is also true that an outsider, by the very fact of his listening, provides stimulation and encouragement. But there is no doubt whatever that whether one is working alone or with an analyst the greatest obstacles to free expression are always within oneself. One is so anxious to ignore certain factors, and to maintain one's image of oneself, that alone or not alone one can hope only to approximate the ideal of free associations. In view of these difficulties the person who is working alone should remind himself from time to time that he acts against his true self-interest if he skips or obliterates any thought or feeling that arises. Also, he should remember that the responsibility is entirely his own: there is no one but himself to guess a missing link or inquire about a gap left open.

This conscientiousness is particularly important in regard to the expression of feelings. Here there are two precepts that should be remembered. One is that the person should try to express what he really feels and not what he is supposed to feel according to tradition or his own standards. He should at least be aware that there may be a wide and significant chasm between genuine feelings and feelings artificially adopted, and should sometimes ask himself—not while associating, but afterward—what he really feels about the matter. The other rule is that he should give as free range to his feelings as

248

he possibly can. This, too, is more easily said than done. It may appear ridiculous to feel deeply hurt at a seemingly trivial offense. It may be bewildering and distasteful to mistrust or hate somebody he is close to. He may be willing to admit a ripple of irritation, but find it frightening to let himself feel the rage that is actually there. He must remember, however, that as far as outside consequences are concerned no situation is less dangerous than analysis for a true expression of feelings. In analysis only the inner consequence matters, and this is to recognize the full intensity of a feeling. This is important because in psychological matters, too, we cannot hang anybody whom we have not first caught.

Of course, no one can forcibly bring forth feelings that are repressed. All anyone can do is not to check those that are within reach. With all the good will in the world Clare, at the beginning of her analysis, could not have felt or expressed more resentment toward Peter than she did. But as her analysis progressed she gradually became more capable of appreciating the existing intensity of her feelings. From one point of view the whole development she went through could be described as a growing freedom to feel what she really felt.

One more word as to the technique of free association: it is essential to abstain from reasoning while associating. Reason has its place in analysis, and there is ample opportunity to use it—afterward. But, as already stressed, the very essence of free association is spontaneity. Hence the person who is attempting it should not try to arrive at a solution by figuring out. Assume, for instance, that you feel so fatigued and so limp that you would like to crawl into bed and pronounce yourself ill. You look out of a second-story window and detect yourself thinking miserably that if you fell down you would at most break an arm. This startles you. You had not known that you were desperate, even so desperate as to want to die. Then you hear a radio turned on above you, and you think with moderate irritation that you would like to shoot the fellow operating it. You conclude rightly that there must be rage as well as despair behind your feeling ill. So far you have done a good job. You already feel less paralyzed, because if you are furious at something you may be able to find the reasons for it. But now you start a frantic conscious search for what might have infuriated you. You go over all the incidents that occurred before you felt so tired. It is possible that you will hit upon the provocation, but the probability is that all your conscious digging comes to nought—and that the real source will *occur* to you half an hour later, after you have become discouraged by the futility of your attempts and have given up the conscious search.

As unproductive as such attempts to force a solution is the procedure of a person who, even while he lets his mind run freely, tries to get at the meaning of his associations by putting two and two together. Whatever prompts him to do so, whether it is impatience or a need to be brilliant or a fear of giving way to uncontrolled thoughts and feelings, this intrusion of reason is bound to disturb the relaxed condition necessary for free association. It is true that the meaning of an association may dawn upon him spontaneously. Clare's series of associations ending with the text of the religious song is a good example of this: here her associations showed an increasing degree of lucidity although no conscious effort had been made to understand them. In other words, the two processes—self-expression and understanding—may sometimes coincide. But as far as conscious efforts are concerned they should be kept strictly separate.

If a definite distinction is thus established between freely associating and understanding, when does one stop associating and try to understand? Fortunately there are no rules whatever. As long as thoughts flow freely there is no sense in arresting them artificially. Sooner or later they will be stopped by something stronger than themselves. Perhaps the person arrives at a point where he feels curious about what it all may mean. Or he may suddenly strike an emotional chord that promises to shed light on something that is troubling him. Or he may simply run out of thoughts, which may be a sign of resistance but also may indicate that he has exhausted the subject for the time being. Or he may have only a limited time at his disposal and still want to try himself at interpreting his notes.

As for the understanding of associations, the range of themes and combinations of themes that they may present is so infinite that there cannot possibly be any fixed rules regarding the meaning of individual elements in individual contexts. Certain fundamental principles have been discussed in the chapter on the share of the

251

analyst in the analytical process. But by necessity much is left to personal ingenuity, alertness, and concentration. I shall therefore merely amplify what has already been said by adding a few remarks on the spirit in which interpretation should be undertaken.

 When a person stops associating and begins to go over his notes in order to understand them, his method of work must change. Rather than being entirely passive and receptive to whatever emerges, he becomes active. Now his reason comes into play. But I should prefer to express it negatively: he no longer excludes reason. Even now he does not use it exclusively. It is difficult to describe with any accuracy the attitude he should adopt when he tries to grasp the meaning of a series of associa· tions. The process should certainly not degenerate into a mere intellectual exercise. If he wants that he will do better to play chess or predict the course of world politics or take to crossword puzzles. An effort to figure out completely rounded interpretations, not missing any possible connotation, may gratify his vanity by proving the superiority of his brains but will scarcely take him much closer to a real understanding of himself. Such an effort even entails a certain danger, for it may hamper progress by engendering a smug know-it-all feeling while in reality he has only catalogued items without being touched by anything.

The other extreme, a merely emotional insight, is far more valuable. If it is not further elaborated this is not ideal either, because it allows many significant leads, not yet altogether lucid, to drop out of sight. But, as we have seen from Clare's analysis, an insight of this kind may set something going. Early in her work she experienced an intense lost feeling in connection with her dream of the foreign city; it was mentioned then that although it is impossible to prove whether this emotional experience had any effect upon the further analysis, through its disquieting nature it may well have loosened her rigid tabu against touching any of the complex ties that fastened her to Peter. Another instance occurred during Clare's final battle with her dependency, when she felt her defiance against taking her life into her own hands; she had then no intellectual grasp of the meaning of this emotional insight, yet it helped her to get out of a state of lethargic helplessness.

Instead of wanting to produce a scientific masterpiece, the person who is working alone should let his interpretation be directed by his interest. He should simply go after what arrests his attention, what arouses his curiosity, what strikes an emotional chord within him. If he is flexible enough to let himself be guided by his spontaneous interest he can be reasonably certain that he will intuitively select those subjects which at the time are most accessible to his understanding, or which fall in line with the problem on which he is working.

I suppose this advice will arouse certain doubts. Do I not advocate too great a leniency? Will the person's interest not lead him to pick out subjects that are familiar to him? Would this course not mean giving in to his resistances? I shall discuss in a separate chapter the question of dealing with resistances. Only this much here. It

253

is true that to be guided by one's interest means to take the way of least resistance. But the *least* resistance is not the same as *no* resistance. The principle means essentially a pursuit of those subjects which at the time being are least repressed. And this is exactly the principle that the analyst applies when he metes out interpretations. As already emphasized, he will choose those factors for interpretation which he believes the patient can fully grasp at the time, and he will refrain from embarking upon problems that are still deeply repressed.

Clare's whole self-analysis illustrates the validity of this procedure. With apparent insouciance she never bothered to tackle any problem that did not elicit a response in her, though it might almost stare her in the face. Without knowing anything about the principle of guidance through interest she intuitively applied it throughout her work, and it served her well. One example may stand for many. In the series of associations ending with the first emergence of the daydream of the great man Clare recognized merely the role that the need for protection played in her relationships. The suggestions concerning her other expectations of men she discarded entirely, though they were an obvious and prominent part of the daydream. This intuitive choice took her on the best course she could have followed. By no means did she merely move on familiar ground. The finding that a need for protection was an integral part of her "love" was a discovery of a factor hitherto unknown. Furthermore, as will be remembered, this discovery constituted the first inroad on her cherished illusion of "love," in itself a painful and incisive step. To have taken up at the same time the aggravating problem of her sponging attitude on men would certainly have been too hard, unless she had dealt with it in a superficial way. This brings up a last point: it is not possible to absorb more than one important insight at a time. An attempt to do so will be detrimental to both, or all, of them. Any relevant insight needs time and undivided concentration if it is to "sink in" and take root.

The understanding of a series of associations demands flexibility not only in the direction of work, as just discussed, but also in the method of approach. In other words, in the selection of problems one must be guided by spontaneous emotional interests as well as by intelligence; and also in the study of the problems that arise one must pass easily from deliberate thinking to intuitive grasping of connections. This latter requirement might be compared to the attitude required in studying a painting: we think about composition, color combinations, brush strokes, and the like, but we also consider the emotional responses that the painting elicits in us. This corresponds, too, to the attitude an analyst adopts toward the patient's associations. While listening to a patient I sometimes do hard thinking about possible meanings, and sometimes I arrive at a conjecture merely by letting the patient's talk play on my intuitive faculties. The verification of any finding, however, no matter how one has arrived at it, always demands full intellectual alertness.

A person may find, of course, that in a series of as-

255

sociations nothing commands his particular interest; he merely sees one or another possibility but nothing illuminating. Or, at the opposite extreme, he may find that even as he delves into one connection certain other elements also strike him as noteworthy. In both instances he will do well to put down in the margin the questions left open. Perhaps at a future time, in going over his notes, the mere theoretical possibilities will mean something more to him, or the shelved questions can be taken up in more detail.

There is still a last pitfall to be mentioned: never accept more than you really believe. This danger is greater in regular analysis, especially if the patient is one who tends to comply with authoritative assertions. But it may play a part also when a person relies on his own resources. He may feel obliged, for instance, to accept whatever "bad" things emerge concerning himself, and to suspect a "resistance" if he hesitates to do so. But he will be on much safer ground if he regards his interpretation as merely tentative, and does not try to convince himself that it is definite. The essence of analysis is truthfulness, and this should extend also to acceptance or nonacceptance of interpretations.

The danger of making an interpretation that is misleading or at least unprofitable can never be excluded, but one should not be overawed by it. If one does not weaken, but carries on in the right spirit, a more profitable path will open up sooner or later, or one will become aware of being in a blind alley and perhaps even learn from that experience. Clare, for instance, before em-

256

barking on her analysis of the dependency, had spent a couple of months digging after an alleged need to have her own way. From the data that emerged later we can understand how she was led in that direction. She told me, though, that during these attempts she had never had a feeling of conviction remotely similar to those she experienced later, during the period reported. Also, the ultimate reason why she had taken that earlier course was that Peter often reproached her for being dominating. This illustrates two points made above: the importance of following one's own interests; and the importance of not accepting anything without full conviction. But while this early search of Clare's meant a waste of time it petered out without harm and did not prevent her from doing highly constructive work afterward.

The constructive character of Clare's work was due not only to the essential correctness of her interpretations but also to the fact that her analysis in this period showed a remarkable degree of continuity. Without intending to concentrate on one problem—for a long time she did not even know what it was—everything she embarked upon turned into a contribution to the problem of her dependency. This unswerving unconscious concentration upon a single problem, which made her approach it relentlessly from ever-new angles, is desirable but rarely attained to the same degree. We can account for it in Clare's case, for at that period she was living under a formidable pressure—how formidable she fully recognized only later—and hence she unconsciously bent all her energies into solving the problems that contributed to it. Such a compelling situation cannot be created artificially. But, the more absorbing one's interest in a problem, the more will a similar concentration be approximated.

Clare's self-analysis illustrates very well the three steps discussed in Chapter Three: recognizing a neurotic trend; understanding its implications; and discovering its interrelations with other neurotic trends. In Clare's analysis, as is often the case, the steps overlapped to some extent: she recognized many of the implications before she finally detected the trend itself. Nor did she make any effort to cover definite steps in her analysis: she did not deliberately set out to discover a neurotic trend, and she did not deliberately examine the connections between her dependency and her compulsive modesty. The recognition of the trend came of itself; and, similarly, the connecting links between the two trends almost automatically became more and more visible as the analytical work proceeded. In other words, Clare did not select the problems—at least not consciously—but the problems came to her, and in their unfolding they displayed an organic continuity.

There was in Clare's analysis a continuity of still another kind, even more important, and more possible to emulate: at no time was there any insight that remained isolated or disconnected. What we see develop is not an accumulation of insights but a structural pattern. Even if every individual insight that a person gains in an analysis is correct, he may still deprive himself of the greatest benefits of his work if the insights remain scattered.

Thus Clare, after recognizing that she let herself be immersed in misery because she secretly believed she could thereby command help, might merely have traced the origin of this trait in childhood and regarded it as a persistent infantile belief. That might have helped some, because nobody really wants to be miserable for no good reason; the next time she found herself succumbing to a spell of misery she might have caught herself up short. But at best this handling of her insight would have diminished in the course of time the gross attacks of exaggerated unhappiness. And these attacks were not the most important expression of the trait. Or she might have gone no further than the next step, of connecting her finding with her actual lack of self-assertion and recognizing that her belief in magic help substituted for an active dealing with life's difficulties. This, although still inadequate, would have helped considerably more, because it would have opened up a new incentive to do away with the whole attitude of helplessness lying behind the belief. But if she had not linked up the magic-help belief with her dependency, and seen the one as an integral part of the other, she could not thoroughly have overcome the belief, because she would always have made the unconscious reservation that if she could only find the permanent "love," help would always be forthcoming. It was only because she saw that connection, and because she recognized the fallacy in such an expectation and the excruciating price she had to pay for it, that the insight had the radically liberating effect it did.

It is thus by no means a matter of purely theoretical interest for a person to discover how a personality trait is embedded in his structure, with manifold roots and manifold effects; it is also of the greatest therapeutic importance. This requirement could be expressed in the familiar terms of dynamics: one must know the dynamics of a trait before one can change it. But this word is like a coin that has become a bit shabby and thin through long usage. Besides, it usually suggests the idea of driving forces, and might be interpreted here to mean that one should merely seek such forces, whether in early childhood or in the present. In this case the notion of dynamics would be misleading, for the influence that a trait exerts on the entire personality is just as important as the factors that determine its existence.

It is by no means only in psychological matters that this awareness of structural interrelations is essential. The considerations I have emphasized apply with equal weight to questions of organic illness, for example. No good physician will regard a heart disorder as an isolated phenomenon. He will consider also in what way the heart is influenced by other organs, such as the kidneys and the lungs. And he must know how the heart condition in turn affects other systems in the body: how it affects, for instance, the circulation of the blood or the action of the liver. His knowledge of such influences will help him to understand the intensity of the disorder.

If it is thus essential in analytic work not to become

lost in scattered details, how can the desirable continuity be brought about? Theoretically the answer is implied in the preceding paragraphs. If a person has made a pertinent observation or gained an insight into himself he should examine how the peculiarity uncovered manifests itself in various areas, what consequences it has and which factors in his personality account for it. But this may be regarded as a rather abstract statement, and therefore I shall try to illustrate it with a constructed example. It must be borne in mind, however, that any brief example necessarily gives an impression of a neatness and a simplicity that do not exist in actuality. Also, such an example, intended to show the variety of factors to be recognized, cannot indicate the emotional experiences a person has when analyzing himself, and thereby it draws a one-sided and overrational picture.

Bearing in mind these reservations, let us imagine a person who has observed that in certain situations in which he would like to participate in discussions he is tongue tied because he is afraid of possible criticism. If he allows this observation to take root within himself he will begin to wonder about the fear involved, since it is out of proportion to any real danger. He will wonder why the fear is so great that it prevents him not only from expressing his thoughts but also from thinking clearly. He will wonder whether the fear is greater than his ambition, and whether it is greater than any considerations of expediency, which, for the sake of his career, would make it desirable that he produce a good impression.

Having thus gained an interest in his problem, he will try to find whether similar difficulties operate in other areas of his life, and, if so, what form they take. He will examine his relations with women. Is he too timid to approach them because they might find fault with him? What about his sexual life? Was he once impotent for a while because he could not get over a failure? Is he reluctant to go to parties? What about shopping? Does he buy an expensive whisky because otherwise the salesman might think he is too economical? Does he tip too generously because the waiter might look down upon him? Furthermore, exactly how vulnerable is he in regard to criticism? What is sufficient to touch off an embarrassment or to make him feel hurt? Is he hurt only when his wife overtly criticizes his necktie or is he uneasy when she merely praises Jimmy for always matching his tie and his socks?

Such considerations will give him an impression of the extent and intensity of his difficulty and of its various manifestations. He will then want to know how it affects his life. He knows already that it makes him inhibited in many areas. He cannot assert himself; he is too compliant with what others expect of him, and therefore he can never be himself but must automatically play a part. This makes him resentful against others, for they appear to dominate him, but it also lowers his own self-esteem.

Finally, he looks out for the factors that are responsible for the difficulty. What made him so fearful of criticism? He may remember that his parents held him to very rigid standards, and may recall any number of incidents in which he was scolded or made to feel inadequate. But he will also have to think of all the weak spots in his actual personality which, in their totality, render him dependent on others and therefore make him regard their opinion of him as of compelling importance. If he can find the answers to all such questions his recognition that he is afraid of criticism will no longer be an isolated insight but he will see the relationship of this trait to the whole structure of his personality.

It may well be asked whether I mean by this example that a person who has discovered a new factor should deliberately ransack his experiences and feelings in the various ways indicated. Certainly not, because such a procedure would involve the same danger of a merely intellectual mastery that was discussed before. But he should grant himself a period of contemplation. He should meditate on his finding in much the same manner as an archaeologist who has discovered a buried statue, badly mutilated, looks at his treasure from all angles until the original features reveal themselves to his mind. Any new factor that a person recognizes is like a searchlight turned on certain domains of his life, lighting up spots which have hitherto been dark. He is almost bound to see them if only he is vividly interested in recognizing himself. These are points at which the guidance of an expert would be particularly helpful. At such times an analyst would actively help the patient to see the significance of the finding, raising one or another question that it suggests and tying it up with previous findings. When no such outside help is available the best thing to do is to refrain from rushing on with the analysis, to remember that a new insight means a conquest of new territory, and to try to benefit from that conquest by consolidating its gains. In each of the examples in the chapter on occasional self-analysis I mentioned questions that might have been suggested by the insight gained. We can be fairly certain that the reason why the people concerned did not hit upon these questions was solely that their interest ended with the removal of their immediate difficulties.

If Clare were asked how she achieved such a remarkable continuity in her analysis she would probably give much the same answer as that given by a good cook when asked for a recipe. His answer usually boils down to the fact that he goes by his feelings. But in the case of analysis this answer is not so unsatisfactory as in the case of an omelette. No one can borrow Clare's feelings, but everyone has feelings of his own by which he can go. And this brings us back to a point made above in discussing the interpretation of associations: it is helpful to have some knowledge of what to look out for, but the looking should be directed by one's own initiative and interest. One should accept the fact that one is a living being driven by needs and interests, and drop the illusion that one's mind operates with a well-greased, machinelike perfection. In this process, as in so many others, thoroughness in penetrating to one or another implication counts more than completeness. The implications that are missed will turn up at some later time when one is perhaps more ready to see them.

Continuity of work is likely to be disturbed also by causes outside a person's control. He must expect interruptions, because he does not live in an experimental vacuum. Any number of daily experiences will encroach upon his thinking, some of them perhaps eliciting emotional responses that call for immediate clarification. Suppose, for instance, that Clare had lost her job while she was working at the problem of her dependency, or that she had assumed a new position requiring more initiative, assertion, and leadership. In either case other problems than her dependency would have stepped into the foreground. All anyone can do in such circumstances is to take these interruptions in his stride and to deal with the problems arising as best he can. He may just as well, however, have experiences that help him with the problem at hand. Thus Peter's breaking of the relationship certainly stimulated Clare to do further analytical work at her problem.

On the whole, there is no need to worry too much about outside interferences. I have found in working with patients that even decisive outside events deflect the course of analysis only for a short while. Rather swiftly, and often without knowing it, the patient swings back to the problem on which he was working, resuming it sometimes at exactly the point where he had left it. We need not resort to any mysterious explanation for this occurrence, such as an assumption that that problem appeals more to the patient than happenings in the outside world. It is more likely that since most experiences can elicit a number of responses, that one which is closest to the problem at hand will touch him most deeply and thereby lead him to retrieve the thread he was about to abandon.

The fact that these remarks have emphasized subjective factors rather than presenting clear-cut directions may recall the criticism raised against analysis that it is more an artistic than a scientific procedure. A discussion of this argument would lead us too far astray because it would involve a philosophical clarification of terms. What counts here is a practical consideration. If analysis is called an artistic activity this would suggest to many people that one must be especially gifted to undertake it. Naturally, our endowments differ. And just as some people are particularly skillful in mechanical matters or have a particularly clear vision for politics, others have a special flair for psychological thinking. Yet what really matters is not an enigmatic artistic endowment but a strictly definable factor—which is one's interest or incentive. This remains a subjective factor, but is it not the decisive one for most of the things we do? What matters is the spirit and not the rules.

CHAPTER TEN

Dealing with Resistances

Analysis sets going or accentuates a play of forces within the self between two groups of factors with contrasting interests. The interest of the one group is to maintain unchanged the illusions and the safety afforded by the neurotic structure; that of the other group is to gain a measure of inner freedom and strength through over-throwing the neurotic structure. It is for this reason that analysis, as has already been strongly emphasized, is not primarily a process of detached intellectual research. The intellect is an opportunist, at the service of whatever interest carries the greatest weight at the time. The forces that oppose liberation and strive to maintain the *status quo* are challenged by every insight that is capable of jeopardizing the neurotic structure, and when thus challenged they attempt to block progress in one way or another. They appear as "resistances" to the analytical work, a term appropriately used by Freud to denote everything that hampers this work from within.

Resistance is by no means produced only by the analytical situation. Unless we live under exceptional conditions life itself is at least as great a challenge to the neurotic structure as is the analyst. A person's secret claims on life are bound to be frequently frustrated because of their absolute and rigid character. Others do not share his illusions about himself, and will hurt him by questioning or disregarding them. Inroads upon his elaborate but precarious safety measures are unavoidable. These challenges may have a constructive influence, but also he may react to them—as he does in analysis—first with anxiety and anger, one or the other prevailing, and then with a reinforcement of the neurotic tendencies. He becomes still more withdrawn, more dominating, more dependent, as the case may be.

In part the relationship with the analyst produces much the same feelings and responses as the relationships with others. But, since analysis is an explicit attack on the neurotic structure, the challenge it presents is greater.

In the major part of analytical literature it is an implicit or explicit axiom that we are helpless toward our resistances, that is, that we cannot overcome them without expert help. This conviction will be held as the strongest argument against the idea of self-analysis. And it is an argument that will carry heavy weight, not only with analysts but also with every patient who has been analyzed, because both analyst and patient know the tenacious and devious struggles that arise when precarious territory is approached. But an appeal to experience can never be a conclusive argument, because experience itself is determined by the whole complex of ruling concepts and customs, and by our mentality. More specifically, analytical experience is determined by the fact that the patient is not given a chance to cope alone with his resistances.

A stronger consideration is the theoretical premise that underlies the analyst's conviction, which is no more and no less than Freud's whole philosophy of the nature of man. This subject is too intricate to delve into here. Only this much: if man is driven by instincts and if among them a destruction instinct plays a prominent role—as was the contention of Freud—not much, if any, space is left in human nature for constructive forces that might strive toward growth and development. And it is these constructive forces that constitute the dynamic counterpole to the forces producing the resistances. A denial of them must by necessity lead to a defeatist attitude toward the possibility of overcoming our resistances through our own efforts. I do not share this part of the Freudian philosophy, but I do not deny that the question of resistance remains a serious consideration. The outcome of self-analysis, as of every analysis, depends by and large on the strength of the resisting forces and the strength of the self to deal with them.

The extent to which a person is factually helpless toward resistances depends not only on their overt but also on their hidden strength—in other words, the degree to which they are discernible. To be sure, they may be discovered and met in open battle; a patient may be fully aware, for example, that he has a resistance against coming to analysis, or he may even realize that he is fighting tooth and nail against relinquishing a neurotic trend, as Clare did in her eventual battle for and against her dependency. More often resistances sneak up on him in disguised forms, without his recognizing them as such. In that case he does not know that resisting forces are operating; he is merely unproductive, or feels listless, tired, discouraged. And he is, of course, helpless when he is thus confronted with an enemy which is not only invisible but, as far as he knows, does not even exist.

One of the most important reasons why he may not recognize the presence of a resistance is the fact that defensive processes are set in motion not only when he is directly confronted with the problems involved, that is, when his secret claims on life are laid bare, his illusions questioned, his security measures jeopardized, but also when he remotely approaches these domains. The more intent he is on keeping them intact, the more sensitive he is to an approach even from the far distance. He is like a person who is frightened by thunderstorms and who is not only terrified by thunder and lightning but reacts with apprehension even to a cloud that appears on the far horizon. These long-distance reactions escape attention so easily because they arise with the emergence of a subject that is apparently innocuous, one that does not seem likely to stir up strong feelings of any kind.

An ability to recognize resistances demands some definite knowledge of their sources and their expressions. Hence it appears appropriate to recapitulate all that has been said about the subject in scattered places throughout the book—often without explicitly mentioning the term "resistance"—and to add certain points that are of special interest for self-analysis.

The sources of resistance are the sum total of a person's interests in maintaining the *status quo*. These interests are not—and emphatically not—identical with a wish to remain ill. Everyone wants to get rid of handicaps and suffering, and in that wish he is all for change, and for a quick change at that. What he wants to maintain is not "the neurosis" but those aspects of it which have proved to be of immense subjective value to him and which in his mind hold the promise of future security and gratification. The basic factors that no one wants to modify one iota are, briefly, those that concern his secret claims on life, his claims for "love," for power, for independence and the like, his illusions about himself, the safety zones within which he moves with comparative ease. The exact nature of these factors depends on the nature of his neurotic trends. Since the characteristics and dynamics of neurotic trends have already been described, I need not go into further details here.

In professional analysis the provocation for resistance is, in the great majority of cases, something that has occurred in the analysis itself. If strong secondary defenses have developed, the first resistances arise as soon as the analyst questions the validity of these defenses, that is, as soon as he casts any doubt on the rightness, goodness, or unalterability of any factor in the patient's personality. Thus a patient whose secondary defenses consist in regarding everything concerning himself, faults included, as excellent and unique will develop a feeling of hopelessness as soon as any motivation of his is questioned. Another patient will react with a mixture of irritability and discouragement as soon as he encounters, or the analyst points out to him, any trace of irrationality within himself. It is in accordance with the function of the secondary defenses—protection of the whole system developed—that these defensive reactions are elicited not merely when a special repressed factor is in danger of being uncovered but when anything is questioned, regardless of content.

But if the secondary defenses are not of such vital strength, or if they have been uncovered and faced, resistances are for the most part a response to attacks on specific repressed factors. As soon as any domain is approached, closely or remotely, which is tabu for the particular patient he will react emotionally with fear or anger and will automatically set going a defensive action in order to prevent further trespassing. This encroachment on a tabu need not be a specific attack but may result merely from the analyst's general behavior. Anything he does or fails to do, says or fails to say, may hurt one of the patient's vulnerable spots and create a conscious or unconscious resentment which for the time being blocks the co-operative work.

But resistances to analytical work can be elicited also

272

by factors outside the analytical situation. If outside circumstances change during analysis in such a way as to favor a smooth functioning of the neurotic trends, or even to render them positively useful, the provocation for resistance is greatly increased; the reason is, of course, that the forces opposing change have been strengthened. But resistance can be provoked also by unfavorable developments in daily life. If a patient feels, for example, that he has been unfairly dealt with by someone in his circle his indignation may be so great that he refuses any effort in analysis to seek the real reason why he felt injured or insulted, his entire energy being concentrated on revenge. In other words, a resistance may be produced by developments outside as well as within the analytical situation if a repressed factor is touched upon, either specifically or remotely.

In principle the provocations for resistance are the same in self-analysis. Here, however, it is not the analyst's interpretations but the person's own encroachment on a painful insight or implication that provokes a resistance. Furthermore, the provocation that may lie in the analyst's behavior is lacking. This is an advantage of self-analysis to some extent, though it should not be forgotten that these provocations can prove to be most constructive if the responses to them are correctly analyzed. Finally, in self-analysis the experiences of daily life seem to have a greater power to produce a blockage. This is readily understandable: in professional analysis the patient's emotions are largely concentrated on the analyst, because of the importance he has assumed for the time being, but such a concentration is lacking when analysis is undertaken alone.

The ways in which resistances express themselves in professional analysis may be roughly grouped under three headings: first, an open fight against the provoking problem; second, defensive emotional reactions; and third, defensive inhibitions or evasive maneuvers. Different though they are in form, essentially these various expressions merely represent different degrees of directness.

In illustration let us assume that with a patient who has a compulsive striving for absolute "independence" the analyst starts to tackle his difficulties in relationships with people. The patient feels this approach as an indirect attack upon his aloofness and therefore on his independence. In this he is right because any work at the difficulties he has with people is meaningful only if the ultimate goal is to improve his human relationships, to help him toward a greater friendliness and a feeling of solidarity with others. The analyst may not even have these goals consciously in mind; he may believe that he merely wants to understand the patient's timidity, his provocative behavior, his predicaments with women. But the patient senses the approaching danger. His resistance may then take the form of an open refusal to tackle the difficulties mentioned, a frank declaration that he does not want to be bothered with people anyhow. Or he may react with distrust of the analyst, suspecting that the latter wants to impose his standards upon him; he may believe, for instance, that the analyst wants to impose on him a distasteful gregariousness. Or he may simply become listless toward the analytical work: he is late for his appointment, nothing much occurs to him, he changes the subject, he has no more dreams, he swamps the analyst with dreams so involved that their meaning is unintelligible.

The first type of resistance, the open fight, is sufficiently clear and familiar to need no elaboration. The third type, defensive inhibitions or tactics of evasion, will be discussed presently in regard to its relevance for self-analysis. But the second type, defensive emotional reactions, is particularly significant in professional analysis, for there such reactions can be concentrated on the analyst.

There are several ways in which a resistance may express itself in emotional reactions regarding the analyst. In the example just mentioned the patient reacted with a suspicion that he was being misled. In others the reaction may be an intense but vague fear of being injured by analysis. Or it may be only a diffuse irritation, or a contempt for the analyst on the grounds that he is too stupid to understand or to help. Or it may take the form of a diffuse anxiety which the patient tries to allay by striving for the analyst's friendship or love.

The startling intensity that these reactions sometimes assume is due in part to the fact that the patient feels threatened in something essential to the structure he has built, but it is due also to the strategical value of the reactions themselves. Such reactions serve to shift the emphasis from the essential job of finding causes and effects

275

to the much safer business of an emotional situation with the analyst. Instead of going after his own problem the patient concentrates his efforts on convincing the analyst, winning him over, proving him wrong, thwarting his endeavors, punishing him for having intruded into territory that is tabu. And along with this shift of emphasis the patient either blames the analyst for all his difficulties, convincing himself that he cannot progress with anyone who treats him with so little understanding and fairness, or puts all responsibility for the work on the analyst, becoming himself inert and unresponsive. Needless to add, these emotional battles may go on under cover, and it may take a great deal of analytical work to bring them to the patient's awareness. When they are thus repressed only the resulting blockage makes itself felt.

In self-analysis resistances express themselves in the same three ways, but with an inevitable difference. Clare's self-analysis produced only once an open and direct resistance, but it produced a great deal of diversified inhibition toward the analytical work and much evasive maneuvering. Occasionally Clare felt a conscious emotional reaction to her analytical findings—such as her shock at discovering her sponging attitude toward men—but such reactions did not prevent her further work. And I believe that this is a fairly typical picture of the way resistances operate in self-analysis. At any rate, it is a picture that we might reasonably expect. Emotional reactions to the findings are bound to occur: the person will feel apprehensive, ashamed, guilty, or irritated about what he discovers in himself. But these reactions do not assume the proportions they do in professional analysis. One reason for this is that there is no analyst with whom he can engage in a defensive fight, or whom he can make responsible: he is thrown back upon himself. Another reason is that he usually deals with himself more gingerly than an analyst would: he will sense the danger far ahead and almost automatically shrink back from a straight approach, resorting instead to one or another means of avoiding the problem for the time being.

This brings us to the defensive inhibitions and evasive maneuvers in which a resistance may express itself. These forms of blocking the way are as innumerable as the variations in personality, and they may develop at any point along the way. Their manifestations in self-analysis can be discussed most conveniently by pointing out certain crucial points at which they may impede progress. In brief summary, they may prevent a person from starting to analyze a problem; they may impair the value of his free associations; they may block his understanding; they may invalidate his findings.

An inhibition toward starting to analyze a problem may be indiscernible, for as a rule a person who is working alone does not analyze himself regularly anyhow. He should not concern himself about the periods in which he feels no need for analysis, though a resistance may be operative in such periods too. But he should be very wary about the times when he feels acutely distressed, disgruntled, fatigued, irritated, indecisive, apprehensive, and nevertheless refrains from any attempt to clarify the condition. He may then feel a conscious reluctance to analyze himself although he is fully aware that by doing so he would at least give himself a chance to get out of the distress and learn something from it. Or he may find any number of excuses for not making the attempt—he is too busy, too tired, there is too little time. This form of resistance is likely to be more frequent in self-analysis than in professional analysis because in the latter, while the patient may forget or cancel an hour occasionally, there is sufficient pressure of routine, politeness, and money to prevent him from doing it very often.

In the process of free association the defensive inhibitions and evasions operate in devious ways. They may make a person flatly unproductive. They may lead him to "figure out" rather than let his mind run freely. They may cause his thoughts to wander off on a tangent, or, rather, produce a kind of dozing off in which he forgets to keep track of the associations that emerge.

A resistance can block his understanding by producing blind spots toward certain factors. Either he will pay no attention to such factors or he will fail to grasp their meaning or significance, even though he is perfectly capable of doing so; there were several examples of this in Clare's analysis. And the feelings or thoughts that emerge may be minimized, as at the beginning Clare minimized her resentment and her unhappiness concerning her relationship with Peter. Furthermore, the resistance may lead to a search in a wrong direction. Here the danger is not so much in being altogether fanciful

278

in the interpretation—that is, reading something into the associations that is not there—as in picking out an existing factor without considering the context in which it appears, and thereby integrating it wrongly. Clare's interpretation of the memory of her doll Emily is an example.

Finally, when a person does arrive at a real finding a resistance operating through inhibitions or evasions can spoil its constructive value in many ways. Perhaps he will invalidate the significance of his finding. Or instead of working at it patiently he may precociously decide that conscious efforts to overcome the particular difficulty are all that is needed. Or he may refrain from following it up, because he "forgets" about it, does not "feel like" doing it, or for some reason or other simply does not get around to doing it. And when it is necessary for him to take a clear stand he may, in conscious good faith, resort to one or another compromise solution and thereby deceive himself about the result he has attained. He will believe then—as Clare did several times—that he has solved a problem though actually he is still far from a solution.

And now, how are resistances to be coped with? To begin with, no one can do anything about those that are unnoticeable, because the first and uppermost requirement is to recognize that a resistance operates. Most resistances can be overlooked, particularly since as a rule one is not too keen to see them. But there are certain forms that are bound to escape attention, no matter how alert one is, or how intent on getting on. The foremost among these are the blind spots and the minimizing of feelings. The severity of the obstacle these present depends upon how widespread and tenacious they are, and on the forces that are behind them. As a rule, they are merely an expression of the fact that one is not yet able to face certain factors. Clare, for instance, could not possibly have seen at the beginning the depth of her resentment against Peter, or the extent to which she suffered under the relationship. Even an analyst could hardly have helped her to see this, or rather to grasp it. Too much work had to be done before she could tackle these factors. This consideration implies, encouragingly, that blind spots will often clear up in time if the work is carried on.

Almost the same holds true for a search in a wrong direction. A resistance that expresses itself in this form is also difficult to detect, and it will cause a loss of time. But its presence may be suspected if one finds after a while that no progress has been made, or that one is only moving in circles in spite of having worked at the problems concerned. It is important in self-analysis—as in any analysis—not to be deluded about the progress made. Such a delusion may lift one's spirits for a while but it easily prevents the discovery of a deep-seated resistance. This possibility of a wrong integration of findings is one of the reasons why an occasional checkup with an analyst is desirable.

The other kinds of resistance are more easily noticed —with due allowance for the fact that they may be of a forbidding intensity. A person can certainly notice his resistance to starting work, if the situation is as described above. In the process of association he can become aware that he is figuring out instead of thinking spontaneously; he can notice that his thoughts are wandering off, and then either retrospectively recall their sequence or at least retrieve the point at which they wandered off. He can catch himself up on fallacious reasoning if he goes over his notes on another day, as Clare did in connection with her expectations of magic help. He can suspect that something is blocking progress if he finds that with conspicuous regularity his findings are highly complimentary, or highly uncomplimentary, to himself. He can even suspect that a reaction of discouragement is a form of resistance, though this is difficult if he is in the clutches of such a feeling; what he should do here is to regard the discouragement itself as a reaction to the analysis, instead of taking it at its face value.

When he has become aware of an existing blockage he should drop whatever analytical pursuits he is engaged in and take the resistance as the most urgent problem to be tackled. It is as useless to force himself to go on against the resistance as it would be, to use Freud's illustration, to try again and again to light an electric bulb that does not burn; one has to see where the electric current is blocked, whether in the bulb, in the fixture, in the cord, in the switch.

The technique of tackling a resistance is to try to associate to it. But in all resistances occurring during analytical work it is helpful, before associating, to go over the notes that precede the blockage, because there is a fair chance that the clue for it lies in an issue at least touched upon, and that while glancing over the notes the point of departure may become evident. And sometimes a person will not be capable of going after a resistance immediately: he may be too reluctant or feel too uneasy to do so. It is advisable then, instead of forcing himself, merely to make a note that at this or that point he suddenly felt uneasy or tired, and to resume work the next day when he may have a fresh perspective on matters.

In advocating that he "associate to a resistance" I mean that he should consider the particular manifestation of the blockage and let his thoughts run freely along that line. Thus if he has noticed that no matter what problems are concerned his interpretations always make him come out on top he should try to take that finding as a point of departure for further associations. If he has become discouraged at a finding he should remember that the latter may have touched upon factors that he is not yet able or willing to change, and try to associate with that possibility in mind. If his difficulty is in starting to analyze, though he feels a need for self-examination, he should remind himself that a previous piece of analysis or some outside occurrence may have produced a blockage.

These resistances provoked by outside factors are particularly common in self-analysis, for reasons that were mentioned above. A person who is in the grip of neurotic trends—or for that matter almost any person—is quite likely to feel offended or unfairly dealt with by a special individual, or by life in general, and to take at face value his reaction of hurt or resentment. In such situations it takes a considerable degree of clarity to distinguish between a real and an imagined offense. And even if the offense is real it need not necessarily produce such reactions: if he is not himself vulnerable to what others may do to him there are many offenses to which he may respond with pity or disapproval of the offender, perhaps with open battle, rather than with hurt or resentment. It is much easier merely to feel a right to be angry than to examine exactly what vulnerable spot in himself has been hit. But for his own interests this is the way he should proceed, even if there is no doubt that the other has been cruel, unfair, or inconsiderate.

Let us assume that a wife is deeply disturbed at learning that her husband has had a transient affair with another woman. Even months later she cannot get over it, although she knows it is a matter of the past and although the husband does everything to re-establish a good relationship. She makes herself and him miserable, and now and then goes on a spree of bitter reproaches against him. There are a number of reasons that might explain why she feels and acts in this way, quite apart from a genuine hurt about the breach of confidence. It may have hurt her pride that the husband could be attached to anyone but herself. It may be intolerable to her that the husband could slip out from her control and domination. The incident may have touched off a dread of desertion, as it would in a person like Clare. She may be discontented with the marriage for reasons of which she is not aware, and she may use this conspicuous occurrence as an excuse for expressing all her repressed grievances, thus engaging merely in an unconscious campaign of revenge. She may have felt attracted toward another man and resent the fact that her husband indulged in a freedom that she had not allowed herself. If she examined such possibilities she might not only improve the situation considerably but also gain a much clearer knowledge of herself. Neither result is possible, however, as long as she merely insists upon her right to be angry. The situation would be essentially the same if she had repressed her anger, though in that case it would be much more difficult to detect her resistance toward self-examination.

A remark may be in place about the spirit of tackling resistances. We are easily tempted to be annoyed at ourselves for having a resistance, as if it indicated an irritating stupidity or obstinacy. Such an attitude is understandable because it is annoying or even exasperating to encounter self-made obstacles on our way to a goal that we desire in our best interests. Nevertheless there is no justification or even any meaning in a person scolding himself for his resistances. He is not to blame for the development of the forces behind them, and, besides, the neurotic trends that they try to protect have given him a means of dealing with life when all other means have failed. It is more sensible for him to regard the opposing forces as given factors. I am almost inclined to say that he should respect them as a part of himself—respect them not in the sense of giving them approval and indulgence but in the sense of acknowledging them as organic developments. Such an attitude will not only be more just to himself but will also give him a much better basis for dealing with resistances. If he approaches them with a hostile determination to crush them he will hardly have the patience and willingness necessary for their understanding.

If resistances are tackled in the way and in the spirit indicated, there is a good chance that they may be understood and overcome—provided they are no stronger than one's constructive will. Those that are stronger present difficulties that can at best be overcome only with expert help.

CHAPTER ELEVEN

Limitations of Self-Analysis

The distinction between resistance and limitation is merely one of degree. Any resistance, if strong enough, can turn into an actual limitation. Any factor that decreases or paralyzes a person's incentive to come to grips with himself constitutes a possible limitation to self-analysis. I do not see any other way of presenting these factors than to discuss them separately, although they are not separate entities. Thus in the following pages the same factor is sometimes dealt with from several viewpoints.

To begin with, a deep-rooted feeling of resignation constitutes a serious limitation to self-analysis. A person may be so hopeless about ever escaping from his psychic entanglements that he has no incentive to make more than a halfhearted attempt to outgrow his difficulties. Hopelessness is present to some extent in every severe neurosis. Whether it constitutes a serious obstacle to therapy depends upon the amount of constructive forces still alive or still to be revived. Such constructive forces are often present even though they seem to have been lost. But sometimes a person has been so entirely crushed at an early age, or has become caught in such unsolvable conflicts, that he has long since given up expectations and struggle.

This attitude of resignation may be entirely conscious, expressing itself in a pervasive feeling of futility concerning one's own life or in a more or less elaborate philosophy of the futility of life in general. Often it is reinforced by a pride in belonging among the few people who have not blinded themselves to this "fact." In some persons no such conscious elaboration has taken place; they are merely passive, endure life in a stoical way, and no longer respond to any prospect of a more meaningful existence.

Such resignation may be hidden also behind a feeling of boredom with life, as in Ibsen's Hedda Gabler. Her expectations are extremely meager. Life should be entertaining now and then, should provide some fun or thrill or excitement, but she expects nothing of positive value. This attitude is often accompanied—as it is in Hedda Gabler—by a profound cynicism, the result of a disbelief in any value in life and in any goal to strive for. But a profound hopelessness may exist also in persons one would not suspect of it, persons who superficially give the impression of being capable of enjoying life. They may be good company, enjoy eating, drinking, sexual relations. In adolescence they may have been promising, capable of genuine interests and genuine feelings. But for some reason or other they have become shallow, have lost their ambition; their interest in work has become perfunctory, their relationships with people are loose, easily made and easily terminated. In short, they, too, have ceased to strive for a meaningful existence and have turned to the periphery of life instead.

Quite a different kind of limitation is set to self-analysis if a neurotic trend is what we might call, with some inaccuracy, too successful. A craving for power, for example, may be gratified to such an extent that the person would scoff at any suggestion of analysis, even though his satisfaction with his life is actually built on quicksand. The same holds true if a longing for dependency is fulfilled in a marriage—a marriage, for example, between such a person and one who has an urge for domination—or in subordination to a group. Similarly, a person may successfully withdraw into an ivory tower and feel comparatively at ease by keeping within its precincts.

This apparently successful assertion of a neurotic trend is produced by a combination of internal and external conditions. As to the former, a neurotic trend that "succeeds" must not conflict too sharply with other needs. Actually a person is never entirely consumed by just one compulsive striving, with everything else blotted out: no human being is ever reduced to a streamlined machine driving in one direction. But this concentration may be approximated. And external conditions

288

must be of a kind to allow such a development. The comparative importance of external and internal conditions varies infinitely. In our society a man who is financially independent can easily withdraw into his ivory tower; but a person with scant resources can also withdraw from the world, if he restricts his other needs to a minimum. One person has grown up in an environment that allows him a display of prestige or power, but another, though he started with nothing, makes such a relentless use of external circumstances that in the end he attains the same goal.

But no matter how such a "successful" assertion of a neurotic trend is achieved, the result is a more or less complete barrier to development by way of analysis. For one thing, the successful trend has become too valuable to be submitted to any questioning. And for another thing, the goal that is striven for in analysis—a harmonious development, with good relations to self and others —would not appeal to such a person because the forces that might respond to the appeal are too enfeebled.

A third limitation to analytical work is constituted by the prevalence of destructive tendencies, whether they pertain primarily to others or to the self. It should be emphasized that such tendencies are not necessarily literally destructive, in the sense of an urge toward suicide, for example. More often they take such forms as hostility or contempt or a general attitude of negation. These destructive impulses are engendered in every severe neurosis. In greater or less degree they are at the bottom of every neurotic development, and they become intensified through the clashing of rigid, egocentric demands and illusions with the external world. Any severe neurosis is like a tight armor that prevents the person from having a full and active life with others. It necessarily engenders a resentment toward life, a deep resentment at being left out which Nietzsche has described as *Lebensneid*. For many reasons hostility and contempt, in regard to self and others alike, may be so strong that to let oneself go to pieces appears as an appealing way to take revenge. To say "no" to everything life has to offer remains the only assertion of self that is left. Ibsen's Hedda Gabler, already mentioned when discussing the factor of resignation, is a good example of a person in whom destructiveness toward others and self is a prevailing tendency.

How prohibitive such destructiveness is to self-development depends, as always, on the degree of severity. If a person feels, for example, that triumph over others is far more important than doing anything constructive with his own life, he is not likely to derive much benefit from analysis. If in his mind enjoyment, happiness, and affection, or any closeness to people, have turned into indications of contemptible softness or mediocrity, it may be impossible for him or anyone else to penetrate his armor of hardness.

A fourth limitation is more comprehensive and more difficult to define, because it concerns the elusive concept of "self." What I mean here is perhaps best indicated by William James's concept of the "real self" as distinguished from the material and social self. In simple terms it concerns what *I* really feel, what *I* really want, what *I* really believe, what *I* really decide. It is, or should be, the most alive center of psychic life. It is this psychic center to which the appeal is made in analytical work. In every neurosis its scope and its aliveness are decreased, for genuine self-regard, native dignity, initiative, the capacity to take responsibility for one's life, and like factors that account for the development of self have always been battered. Moreover, the neurotic trends themselves have usurped a great deal of its energies because—to resume an analogy previously used—they turn a person into an airplane driven by remote control.

In most instances there are sufficient possibilities for recapturing and developing the self, though the strength of these possibilities is difficult to estimate at the beginning. But if the real self is considerably damaged the person has lost his own center of gravity and is directed by other forces, from within or from without. He may overadapt himself to his environment and become an automaton. He may find his only right to existence in being helpful to others, and thus be socially useful though his lack of any center of gravity within himself is bound to hamper his efficiency. He may lose all inner sense of direction, and either drift aimlessly or be entirely directed by a neurotic trend, as mentioned in the discussion of "oversuccessful" neurotic trends. His feelings, thoughts, and actions may be almost entirely determined by an inflated image which he has built up of himself: he will be sympathetic not because he really feels it, but because to be sympathetic is part of his other, apparently equally cynical, who nevertheless feels a positive respect and liking for anyone who lives up to genuine ideals. Or between a person who is diffusely irritable and contemptuous toward people but responds to their friendliness, and one who, like Hedda Gabler, is equally vicious toward friend and enemy, and even tends particularly to destroy those who touch remnants of softer feelings within himself.

If the barriers to self-development through analysis are genuinely unsurpassable it is never one factor alone that accounts for them, but a combination of several. Deep hopelessness, for example, is an absolute obstacle only if it is combined with a reinforcing tendency, an armor of self-righteousness, perhaps, or a pervasive destructiveness; complete alienation from self cannot be prohibitive unless there is also some such reinforcing tendency as a firmly entrenched dependency. In other words, genuine limitations exist only in severe and complicated neuroses, and even there constructive forces may still be alive, if only they can be found and used.

There are various ways in which deterring psychic forces, such as those discussed above, may affect an endeavor at self-analysis, if they are not of such compelling strength as to prohibit the endeavor entirely. For one thing, they may imperceptibly spoil the whole analysis by causing it to be carried out in a spirit of only partial honesty. In these cases the one-sided emphases and the blind spots concerning rather wide areas, which are present at the beginning of every analysis, persist throughout the work, rather than decreasing gradually in extent and intensity. Factors lying outside these areas may be faced squarely. But since no area within the self is isolated from others, and hence cannot really be understood without being related to the whole structure, even those factors that are seen remain on the level of superficial insights.

Rousseau's *Confessions,* though only remotely akin to analysis, may serve as an example of this possibility. Here is a man who apparently wants to give an honest picture of himself, and does so to a moderate extent. But throughout the book he retains blind spots concerning his vanity and his inability to love—to mention only two outstanding factors—which are so blatant that they impress us today as grotesque. He is frank about what he expects and accepts from others, but he interprets the resulting dependency as "love." He recognizes his vulnerability but relates it to his "feeling heart." He recognizes his animosities, but they always turn out to be warranted. He sees his failures, but always others are responsible for them.

To be sure, Rousseau's confessions are not a self-analysis. Yet on rereading the book in recent years I have often been reminded of friends and patients whose analytical endeavors were not too different. The book, indeed, deserves a careful and critical study. An endeavor at self-analysis, even though more sophisticated, may easily meet with a similar fate. A person equipped with greater psychological knowledge might merely be more forces operating in the present personality. For example, the peculiar development that took place in Clare's relationship with her mother had a definite bearing upon her dependency on men. But if Clare had seen only the similarities between the old pattern and the new one she would have failed to recognize the essential driving forces that compelled her to perpetuate the pattern. She might have seen that she subordinated herself to Peter as she had to the mother, that she hero-worshiped Peter as she had adored the mother, that she expected him to protect her and to help her in distress as she had expected the mother to help her, that she resented Peter's rejecting her as she had resented the mother's discrimination against her. In recognizing these connections she might have gained a certain distance to her actual problem, simply by recognizing the operation of a compulsive pattern. But actually she clung to Peter not because he represented a mother-image but because, through her compulsive modesty and through her repressed arrogance and ambition, she had lost her self-regard, almost lost her identity; thus she was fearful, inhibited, defenseless, and isolated, and on these grounds was compelled to seek shelter and restoration of herself in ways that were doomed to failure and merely entangled her more deeply in the network of her inhibitions and fears. Only by realizing these dynamics could she eventually free herself from the aftermaths of an unfortunate childhood.

Still another one-sided emphasis is a tendency to harp always on the "bad" sides, or what are regarded as such. Confessing and condemning can then take the place of understanding. This is done partly in a spirit of hostile self-recrimination but also with a secret belief that confession alone is enough to harvest a reward.

These blind spots and one-sided emphases may be found, of course, in any endeavor at self-analysis, whether or not the limitations discussed above are present. To some extent they may result from mistaken preconceptions about psychoanalysis. In this case they can be corrected if the person achieves a more rounded understanding of psychic processes. But the point I would stress here is that they may also represent merely a means of evading the essential problems. In this case they are ultimately caused by resistances to progress, and if these resistances are strong enough—if they amount to what I have described as limitations—they may constitute a definite obstruction to the success of the analysis.

The deterring forces that were mentioned above can frustrate self-analysis also by causing a premature termination of efforts. I am referring here to instances in which the analysis proceeds up to a certain point, is helpful to some extent, but does not proceed beyond this point because the person will not grapple with those factors within himself which prevent his further development. This may happen after he has overcome the most disturbing factors and no longer feels a pressing need to work at himself, even though many diffuse handicaps are left. The temptation to relax in this way is particularly great if life goes smoothly and offers no particular challenge. Naturally in such situations all of us are less eager for complete self-recognition. And it is ultimately a matter of our personal philosophy of life how highly we value a constructive dissatisfaction with ourselves that drives us on toward further growth and development. It is desirable, however, that we be or become clear as to what exactly are our sets of values, and act accordingly. It would constitute an essential lack of truth to ourselves if, with a conscious adherence to the ideal of growth, in reality we relinquished our efforts to measure up to it or even let them be stifled by a smug self-satisfaction.

But a person may break off his efforts at self-analysis for quite an opposite reason: he has arrived at various relevant insights into his difficulties, but nothing changes and he becomes discouraged by the lack of tangible results. Actually, as mentioned before, the discouragement itself constitutes a problem and should be tackled as such. But if it derives from severe neurotic entanglements—for example, from the attitude of hopeless resignation described above—the person may be unable to cope with it alone. This does not mean that his efforts up to this point have been useless. Very often, despite the limitations to what he can accomplish, he has succeeded in losing one or another gross manifestation of his neurotic difficulties.

Inherent limitations may cause a premature termination of self-analysis in still another way: the person may arrive at a kind of pseudo solution by arranging his life to fit in with his remaining neurosis. Life itself may be instrumental in bringing about such solutions. He may be thrown into a situation that provides an outlet for a craving for power, or permits a life of obscurity and subordination in which he need not assert himself. He may seize the possibility of a marriage to solve his urge for dependency. Or he may more or less consciously decide that his difficulties in human relationships—some of which he has recognized and understood—are too great a drain on his energies, and that the only way to live a peaceful life or to save his creative abilities is to withdraw from others; he may then restrict to a minimum his need for people or for material things, and under these conditions be able to work out a tolerable existence. These solutions are not ideal, to be sure, but a psychic equilibrium may be reached on a better level than before. And in some circumstances of very severe entanglements such pseudo solutions may be the most that can be attained.

In principle these limits to constructive work are present in professional analysis as well as in self-analysis. In fact, as was mentioned before, if the deterring forces are strong enough the idea of analysis will be rejected altogether. And even if it is not rejected—if the person suffers so much under the pressure of his disabilities that he undertakes analytical treatment—the analyst is no sorcerer who can conjure up forces that are entirely choked. There is no doubt, however, that by and large the limitations are considerably greater for self-analysis. In many instances an analyst can liberate constructive forces by showing the patient concrete problems accessible to a solution, whereas if the patient were working alone, and felt blindly caught in invisible and apparently inextricable entanglements, he could not possibly pick up enough courage to grapple with his problems. Moreover, the relative strength of the various psychic forces within the patient may change during treatment, because none of these forces is a quantity given once and for all. Every step that leads him closer to his real self and closer to others renders him less hopeless and less isolated and thereby adds to his active interest in life, including also his interest in his own development. Therefore after a period of common work with an analyst even patients who started with severe neurotic difficulties may in some cases be able to continue on their own, if necessary.

Though on the whole the comparison with professional analysis is in favor of the latter whenever intricate and diffuse entanglements are concerned, there are certain reservations that should be borne in mind. It is not entirely fair to compare self-analysis, and its unavoidable deficiencies, with an ideal analytical treatment. I know several people who were barely touched by treatment but afterward grappled successfully on their own with rather serious problems. We should be cautious both ways, and neither underrate nor overrate what can be done without expert help.

This brings us back to a question that was raised at the beginning, regarding the specific conditions under which a person can analyze himself. If he has already had some analytical treatment, and if conditions are favorable, I believe, as I have emphasized throughout the book, that he can continue alone with the hope of achieving far-reaching results. The example of Clare— and also other cases not presented here—shows clearly that it is possible, with previous experience, to deal alone with even severe and intricate problems. It appears a reasonable hope that both analysts and patients will become more aware of this possibility, and that more attempts of this kind will be made. It may be hoped, too, that analysts will gradually assemble criteria that will enable them to judge when they can reasonably encourage the patient to continue his work independently.

In this context there is a consideration I should like to emphasize, though it does not refer directly to self-analysis. If the analyst does not assume an authoritative attitude toward the patient, but makes it clear from the beginning that the enterprise is a co-operative one in which both analyst and patient work actively toward the same goal, the patient will be able to develop his own resources in a much higher degree. He will lose the paralyzing feeling that he is more or less helpless and that the analyst must carry the sole responsibility, and will learn to respond with initiative and resourcefulness. Broadly speaking, psychoanalytic treatment has developed from a situation in which both patient and analyst are relatively passive to one in which the analyst is more active, and finally to one in which both participants take an active role. Where the latter spirit prevails more can be accomplished in a shorter time. The reason I mention this fact here is not to point out the possibilities of shortening analytical treatment, though neurotic troubles and the ways of tackling them attempts of this kind can be carried further—always provided the severity of the neurosis is not prohibitive. The structure of personality is so much less rigid in milder neurotic entanglements than in severe ones that even attempts that are not carried very far may help considerably. In severe neuroses it is often necessary to do a great deal of analytical work before any liberating effect is achieved. In milder disturbances even a single uncovering of an unconscious conflict may be the turning point toward a freer development.

But even if we grant that a considerable number of people can profitably analyze themselves, will they ever complete the work? Will there not always be problems left that are not solved or not even touched upon? My answer is that there is no such thing as a complete analysis. And this answer is not given in a spirit of resignation. Certainly the greater the degree of transparency and the more freedom we can attain, the better for us. But the idea of a finished human product not only appears presumptuous but even, in my opinion, lacks any strong appeal. Life is struggle and striving, development and growth—and analysis is one of the means that can help in this process. Certainly its positive accomplishments are important, but also the striving itself is of intrinsic value. As Goethe has said in *Faust:*

> Whoe'er aspires unweariedly,
> Is not beyond redeeming.

Norton Paperbacks on Psychiatry and Psychology

Abraham, Karl. *On Character and Libido Development, Six Essays, edited by Bertram D. Lewin, M.D.*

Alexander, Franz. *Fundamentals of Psychoanalysis.*

Alexander, Franz. *Psychosomatic Medicine.*

Brill, A. A. *Freud's Contribution to Psychiatry.*

Cannon, Walter B. *The Wisdom of the Body.*

Erikson, Erik H. *Childhood and Society.*

Erikson, Erik H. *Identity: Youth and Crisis.*

Erikson, Erik H. *Insight and Responsibility.*

Erikson, Erik H. *Young Man Luther.*

Ferenczi, Sandor. *Thalassa: A Theory of Genitality.*

Freud, Sigmund. *An Autobiographical Study.*

Freud, Sigmund. *Civilization and its Discontents.*

Freud, Sigmund. *The Ego and the Id.*

Freud, Sigmund. *Jokes and Their Relation to the Unconscious.*

Freud, Sigmund. *Leonardo da Vinci and a Memory of His Childhood.*

Freud, Sigmund. *New Introductory Lectures on Psychoanalysis.*

Freud, Sigmund. *On Dreams.*

Freud, Sigmund. *On the History of the Psychoanalytic Movement.*

Freud, Sigmund. *An Outline of Psychoanalysis.*

Freud, Sigmund. *The Problem of Anxiety.*

Freud, Sigmund. *The Psychopathology of Everyday Life.*

Freud, Sigmund. *Totem and Taboo.*

Hinsie, Leland E. *The Person in the Body.*

Horney, Karen (Ed.) *Are You Considering Psychoanalysis?*

Horney, Karen. *New Ways in Psychoanalysis.*

Horney, Karen. *The Neurotic Personality of Our Time.*

Horney, Karen. *Our Inner Conflicts.*

Horney, Karen. *Self-Analysis.*

James, William. *Talks to Teachers.*

Kasanin, J. S. *Language and Thought in Schizophrenia.*

Kelly, George A. *A Theory of Personality.*

Klein, Melanie and Joan Riviere. *Love, Hate and Reparation.*

Levy, David M. *Maternal Overprotection.*

Lifton, Robert Jay. *Thought Reform and the Psychology of Totalism.*

Piaget, Jean. *The Child's Conception of Number.*

Piaget, Jean. *The Origins of Intelligence in Children.*

Piaget, Jean. *Play, Dreams and Imitation in Childhood.*

Piaget, Jean and Bärbel Inhelder. *The Child's Conception of Space.*

Ruesch, Jurgen, M.D. and Gregory Bateson. *Communication: The Social Matrix of Psychiatry.*

Sullivan, Harry Stack. *Conceptions of Modern Psychiatry.*

Sullivan, Harry Stack. *The Interpersonal Theory of Psychiatry.*

Wheelis, Allen. *The Quest for Identity.*

Zilboorg, Gregory. *A History of Medical Psychology.*

NORTON BOOKS
in Psychiatry and Psychology

ALEXANDER, FRANZ
  Fundamentals of Psychoanalysis
  Psychoanalysis and Psychotherapy
  Psychosomatic Medicine

ALLEN, FREDERICK H.
  Positive Aspects of Child Psychiatry

COHEN, MABEL BLAKE, ED.
  Advances in Psychiatry

ENGLISH, O. S. and FINCH, STUART M.
  Introduction to Psychiatry, 3rd Edition

ENGLISH, O. S. and PEARSON, G. H. J.
  Common Neuroses of Children and Adults
  Emotional Problems of Living, 3rd Edition

ERIKSON, ERIK H.
  Childhood and Society
  Young Man Luther
  Identity: Youth and Crisis
  Insight and Responsibility

FENICHEL, OTTO
  Collected Papers, First Series
  Collected Papers, Second Series
  The Psychoanalytic Theory of Neurosis

FINCH, STUART M.
  Fundamentals of Child Psychiatry

FREUD, SIGMUND
  An Autobiographical Study
  Civilization and its Discontents
  The Complete Introductory Lectures on Psychoanalysis
  Jokes and Their Relation to the Unconscious
  Leonardo da Vinci and a Memory of His Childhood
  New Introductory Lectures on Psychoanalysis
  On Dreams
  On the History of the Psychoanalytic Movement
  An Outline of Psychoanalysis
  The Problem of Anxiety
  The Psychopathology of Everyday Life
  Totem and Taboo

GRINKER, ROY R.
  Psychosomatic Research

VAN DEN BERG, J. H.
The Changing Nature of Man

WALTER, W. GREY
The Living Brain

WATZLAWICK, PAUL; BEAVIN, JANET; and
JACKSON, DON D.
Pragmatics of Human Communication

WHEELIS, ALLEN
The Quest for Identity

WYSS, DIETER
Depth Psychology

ZILBOORG, GREGORY and HENRY, GEORGE W.
History of Medical Psychology